ENCOUNTERS WITH HOLINESS

John T. Catoir, JCD

ENCOUNTERS WITH HOLINESS

My interviews with:
Mother Teresa of Calcutta
Dorothy Day
Archbishop Fulton J. Sheen
Catherine de Hueck Doherty
Fr. Walter Ciszek, S.J.
Leon-Josef Cardinal Suenens
John Cardinal O'Connor
Mother Angelica
and many others

ST PAULS

Library of Congress Cataloging-in-Publication Data

Catoir, John T.
. Encounters with holiness : my interviews with Mother Teresa of Calcutta, Dorothy Day, Archbishop Fulton J. Sheen, Catherine de Hueck Doherty, Walter Ciszek, Leon-Josef Cardinal Suenens, John Cardinal O'Connor, Mother Angelica, and many others / by John T. Catoir
    p. cm.
  ISBN: 978-0-8189-1237-5
  1. Spiritual life–Catholic Church. 2. Catholics–Religious life. 3. Catholics–Biography. 4. Holiness. 5. Christian saints. I. Title.

BX2350.3.C385 2006
282.092'2–dc22
[B]
    2006025143

Produced and designed in the United States of America by the Fathers and Brothers of the Society of St. Paul,
2187 Victory Boulevard, Staten Island, New York 10314-6603, as part of their communications apostolate.

ISBN: 978-0-8189-1237-5

Printing Information:

Current Printing - first digit   2 3 4 5 6 7 8 9 10

Year of Current Printing - first year shown

2017 2018 2019 2020 2021 2022 2023 2024 2025 2026

With great admiration and respect
I dedicate this book to the founder of The Christophers,
FATHER JAMES KELLER, M.M.

TABLE OF CONTENTS

HOLINESS

Holiness is not something that comes from doing good.
We do good because we are holy.
Holiness is not something we acquire by avoiding evil.
We avoid evil because we are holy.
Holiness is not something that is the result of prayer.
We pray because we are holy.
Holiness is not the by-product of kindness.
We are kind because we are holy.
Holiness is not something that comes from courage.
We are courageous because we are holy.
Holiness is not the result of character building.
We build character because we are holy.
Holiness is not a gift we obtain after a lifetime of service.
We give a lifetime of service because we are holy.
Our holiness is God living in us, Emmanuel,
and while it is true that holiness carries with it
both the cross and the Resurrection,
it is more a gift than a reward.

REFLECTIONS ON HOLINESS

Pope Benedict XVI, at the conclusion of the Synod of Bishops, on October 23, 2005, defined sainthood in this way: *"A saint is someone who is so fascinated by the beauty of God and by his perfect truth that he is progressively transformed by it. For this beauty and this truth he is ready to renounce everything, even himself."*

There are two kinds of saints: the heroes, and the unsung heroes.

John Milton, in his sonnet on blindness, wrote these famous words: *"They also serve who only stand and wait."* The service of love very often takes the form of patient endurance. Among the meek, waiting in quiet desperation is a normal part of life.

In this book I have included many people who are action heroes. I'd like to say a word about those who suffer in silence.

God waits. The world He made is filled with waiting. Waiting is one of the primary laws of nature. Winter waits for spring. The buds wait for warmth. The earth waits for rain. Nothing in life comes to instant maturity. The value of waiting is far superior to mindless activism. All things begin as a tiny seed, waiting to grow to full stature. Waiting gives birth to hope.

Dante described hope as "an expectation with certitude." For those who wait, there will come a new dawn, and *"all manner of things shall be well"* (Julian of Norwich). The ultimate meaning of all our waiting is hidden from our eyes, but as we gradually learn to open ourselves to the Holy Spirit, we also learn to reach into the depths of our own being. Sometimes we find the very peace we seek residing within us.

At times all we can do is just get through the day. Hanging in there when you want to run away might be the holiest thing you will ever be able to do. The courage required in persevering, and doing your duty, can at times be daunting.

For instance, those who are physically and mentally challenged, are among the unsung heroes of our times. They abound in this world, and go unnoticed. They do their best to make the most of what life has handed them, and in the process they often rise to the highest level of heroic virtue.

In the canonization process, heroic virtue is the criteria of sanctity. With this in mind, it seems to me that disabled people, and their caretakers, are among the holiest people on earth. They are the cream of the crop.

I once preached the homily at the funeral Mass of a young man I had known for many years. Oliver, the son of José and Catherine deVinck, was blind, mute, and bed-ridden throughout the entire 33 years of his life. Nevertheless he had a profound impact on everyone who came in contact with him. All of his brothers and sisters are better people because of his presence in their lives. Here is an excerpt from that funeral homily:

> *Life is not thought to be sacred by many people. Evidently not, when you consider that there are over 45 million abortions performed in the world every year. However, Oliver's family regarded his life as a priceless gift, and a sacred trust.*
> *Though Oliver never spoke, I learned so much about him from his meekness and his patient endurance.*

His life reminded me of Tolstoy's short story entitled, "What Men Live By." In a world where money and possessions are regarded as the only real security, this young man gave testimony to the truth that we live by love, at every stage of life. Oliver was rich in love. He was hand-fed every spoonful of food he ever ate. On his deathbed, he was entirely free from bedsores, even though his back never left the sheets beneath him.

He taught me about the deeper meaning of being dependent. By his dependence he served those who took care of him. He helped them to grow in love, wisdom, kindness, patience, perseverance and fidelity.

His life gave a special meaning to the words of Jesus: "What you did for the least of My brethren, you did for Me." *He was the least among us, meek and humble of heart like Jesus. He evoked from others the best that was in them, simply by his total dependence on them.*

He taught me much about innocence. Oliver was pure of heart. He was never jealous, resentful, or deceitful. He never hurt anyone. He kept all the commandments, and in a special way, he excelled in honoring his mother and father.

We usually think that people honor their parents by their accomplishments. Parents take pride in the success of their children: the diplomas, the financial gains, the worldly honors. However, Oliver honored his parents in a different way. He did it by revealing the noble quality of their love. They were the primary carriers of God's love. That is what kept him alive for so long.

And now his life story, 33 years in the making, is over. Oliver is now free of his body. Like the angels in paradise, he is free. And he has all eternity to laugh and play in the fullness of God's joy. That is why on this day of his burial, we can all rejoice and be glad. I am grateful to God for having known Oliver.

There is often a hidden joy in what might appear to be a tragic story. Joy is usually a hidden feature of the life of a saint. We know that the highest level of sanctity is found in a person with a joyful spirit.

St. Paul said: *"Rejoice always, and be grateful in all circumstances, for this is the will of God for you in Christ Jesus"* (1 Thessalonians 5:16-17). He knew that living joyfully would not be easy.

Holiness is God living in you. Holy people stay in touch with God's voice; they abide in His love. They ask God to change them into the person He wants them to be. The challenge of holiness requires humility. The conversations with such people that follow in this book reveal the humility of each and every one of them.

Holy people know that they will accomplish nothing if they try it on their own. As a result they turn their weakness over to God, and depend on Him to do for them what they cannot do for themselves.

As you read the following conversations with some of our most recent saints, you will learn that they all had to turn their lives over to God. They learned to act as if everything depended on them, and at the same time pray as if everything depended on God.

When St. Paul reminds us to *"Rejoice always,"* he challenged us to live our lives joyfully. St. Teresa reformed her inner life, and by God's grace moved away from the inner gloom and doom. She gradually ascended to a higher level of mysticism, one that filled her soul with joy.

This is in keeping with the words of Jesus. At the Last Supper, Jesus spoke these beautiful words, *"I have told you this that your joy may be full."*

One of the most common characteristics of the saints is their spirit of joy. Joy is the infallible sign of the Holy Spirit.

Jesus assured us that His yoke is easy and His burden is light. The goal therefore is to let the Lord do most of the worrying.

Do not be concerned about success or failure. Leave your fears behind. Call on Jesus and His Holy Spirit to help you become an instrument of love and joy. This is our life's work.

Study the saints, and at the same time ask for the grace to discern your own purpose and direction in life.

We all need the help and prayers of the saints to show us the way. With God all things are possible.

One of my favorite saints, St. Cyril of Jerusalem (386 A.D.), was a great teacher of supernatural mysteries. In a marvelous passage, where he compared God's Spirit to the rain falling down from heaven, he clarified for me the mystery of God's universal love.

Taking this quote from Jesus, "*The water that I shall give him will become in him a spring of water welling up to eternal life*" (John 4:14), he explained that "*water comes down from heaven as rain, and although it is always the same in itself, it produces many different effects: one in the palm tree, another in the vine, and so on, throughout the whole of creation. It does not come down, as one thing now, and as another then, but while remaining essentially the same, this water adapts itself to the nature and need of every creature that receives it. In the same way the Holy Spirit, whose nature is always the same, simple and indivisible, apportions grace to each individual person as He wills.*"

The Holy Spirit enhances our natural gifts in mysterious ways, and strengthens our weaknesses in the process. St. Paul said so eloquently, "*In my weakness, I find strength.*" Knowledge of his weakness led him to turn to God for strength.

When human weakness or personal shortcomings prevent us from doing what we would like to do, or being the exceptional person we would like to be, we shouldn't be discouraged. St. Paul once had an identity crisis because of this misunderstanding. He wrote, "*The good that I would do, I never do, and that which I would not do, that I do.*" In spite of his low self-esteem, St. Paul became a great saint once he realized that his weakness didn't matter. He learned to rely on God's strength, not his own.

St. Cyril had more to say on this point:

> *The Holy Spirit makes one person a teacher of divine truth, inspires another to prophesy... The Spirit strengthens one person's self-control, shows another how to help the poor, teaches another to fast and lead a life of asceticism, makes another oblivious to the needs of the body, trains another for martyrdom... In each person the Spirit reveals His presence in a particular way for the common good.*

We are all called to accept the specific gifts God has given us, and to trust in His wisdom about how we will use those gifts, and for what purpose. Knowing that He will nourish our souls with His grace, we make good use of our confusion and frustration. We can learn to wait patiently for Him to show us the way.

It is possible to be weak in many areas, while still being gifted in others. No one receives all the gifts. Yet how many people feel discouraged when they come across real holiness, or outstanding generosity in another? They feel diminished by the comparison. But human weakness is relative, and it is not very important in the great scheme of life. With God as our strength, all things are possible.

As I reflect on the teaching of St. Cyril, I realize how important it is for us to thank God for what we have. During the nearly eighteen years that I was the director of The Christophers in New York City, I promoted the motto: **It's better to light a candle than curse the darkness,** which was taken from a three thousand year old Chinese proverb.

We all have the capacity to light one candle. Some lights are obviously brighter than others, but the combined light of all those who live in the Light makes a magnificent blaze. All of our lights blend, giving a blinding illumination to the world. We are the Body of Christ. He is the Light of the World.

Since the gifts of the Spirit are given for the common good, we can all rejoice in our individual gifts, and share them with others. The Holy Spirit appears everywhere with His grace. All we need to do is cooperate, and let His light flow through us.

Cooperating with God's Grace

Having considered the importance of patience, perseverance and meekness in the pursuit of holiness, it is important to understand that we also need to take responsibility for our own happiness, and our spiritual growth. While it's true that "all is grace," we have a will, which says yes or no. We can make an effort to cooperate with God's grace, or not.

Poor health and moral weakness is not a concern to God. What matters the most in producing rich and abundant good fruit is our willingness to become an instrument of His peace and joy. God uses the weak things of this world to accomplish great things. He draws good from evil.

The way we cooperate with God is key. Dr. Viktor Frankl in his book *The Doctor and the Soul* explains how a mental patient was able to use her will in spite of her condition:

> *How instinctive – though unwittingly and unintentionally so – was the reply that a schizophrenic patient gave to the question of whether she was weak-willed: "I'm weak-willed when I want to be, and when I don't want to be I'm not weak-willed." This psychotic patient was skillfully pointing out that people are inclined to hide their own freedom of will from themselves, by alleging weakness of will.*

Similarly a healthy person might be inclined to say, *"I'm only as interested in giving myself to God as I want to be."* Others might say, *"I'm too weak to be a saint."* If they believe that, it will become a self-fulfilling prophecy.

More often than not people really don't want to submit to God's will, and they hide behind their alleged weakness as an excuse for living as they please. Dr. Frankl calls this approach a form of reconciliation with one's weakness; a way of working with it.

Here's another case in point. Frankl wrote about a woman who suffered from severe acoustic hallucinations. She was continually hearing voices, and the voices put her down constantly, jeering at everything she did. Yet she was able to maintain a cheerful attitude. One day when asked how she managed to keep up her good spirits, she replied: "I just say to myself: *'After all, to hear voices like this is a lot better than being deaf.'"*

Now that's what I call positive thinking. She didn't blame anyone for her mental sickness; she just decided to live with it. It is not the bad things that happen to you in life, it's how you deal with them that makes all the difference.

At every stage of our development we possess the spiritual freedom to choose our own attitude, and consequently our own destiny. The will says "yes" or "no." This function of the human will is to decide. Grace builds on nature. So it is important to accept the will as the center of the human personality.

Emotional forces and subconscious drives do not compel us as much as we think. St. Thomas Aquinas said, *"If you want to be a saint, will it."* He knew that the will is central to the personality. This means that, by God's grace, holiness is really possible even though at times, when we are at our worst, we feel as though it is impossible. Feelings are not facts in these matters.

Father Pierre Teilhard de Chardin was a Jesuit anthropologist, and one of the many saints of the twentieth century who will never be canonized. He interpreted the theory of evolution as originating from a supreme intelligence. He insisted that we are moving and evolving toward this Creator, who is our ultimate purpose and destiny.

Evolution, in his view is God-oriented. He identified God as "the Alpha and the Omega" point of all creation. He went further saying that the purpose of the entire evolutionary process reaches fulfillment in Our Lord Jesus Christ.

We know that the Lord will come again at the end of human history. We also know that Jesus is the center of our spiritual lives. He gives meaning to life itself. Jesus is not only the Lord of every individual person, but also the Lord of history.

Behind the theory of theistic evolution is the belief that men and women are created by God and are works in progress. That means human beings are perfectible. The Church believes in human progress, and we are all part of the colossal struggle to grow in wisdom, age and grace, thus advancing human history to its ultimate purpose, the glory of God.

There is nothing new under the sun. In the spiritual classic, *Abandonment to Divine Providence*, written by another famous Jesuit, Father Jean-Pierre de Caussade, we read: *"The secret of happiness and sanctity rests in our fidelity to the will of God as it is manifested in the duty of the present moment."* He continued: *"The great and solid foundation of the spiritual life is to give oneself to God… in such a way that the good pleasure of God, and his happiness becomes our sole joy and good."*

The Little Flower, St. Thérèse of Lisieux, agreed wholeheartedly. As she lay dying, she made the statement that she performed all her actions in life with a single purpose in mind, namely, *"to make God happy."* She did this by loving Him, and being happy with Him throughout her short life on earth.

Jesus said, *"I have told you all these things that your joy may be full."* He wants us to be happy with Him here and now. We have all been taught that we can offend God by not doing His will, but too few of us understand that we can make God happy by simply being happy with Him. Most people tend to worry about how much we displease God if we do not do His will.

The Little Flower emphasized the importance of trying to make God happy by enjoying our life with Him. It made her happy to approach the spiritual life in this way. In the book, *The Happiness of God: Holiness in Thérèse of Lisieux* (St Pauls/Alba House, 1988) by Susan Leslie, a contemplative nun from Oxford, England, we read: *"Thérèse insists that to be happy is an important way of showing our love for God... He loves a happy soul, one perfectly attuned to Him, content with all He wills or permits. The happy soul has faith in the loving providence of God, even in times of darkness and perplexity."*

A happy soul is attuned to God's happiness, being content with all that He wills or permits. It would be wonderful if our good people could move beyond themselves, and see the profound value of this spiritual outlook. So many people are full of fear and doubt. They become skeptical as they see the world they inherited as full of turmoil and danger. What we need to teach them is that skepticism, pessimism and fear are not from God. The Lord said, *"Do not be afraid."*

The saints are people who know how to trust the Lord, and that is how they achieve peace of mind. Everyone has to trust someone. We cannot discard the wisdom of the prophets. Once again I return to the spiritual classic, *Abandonment to Divine Providence*, where Fr. Jean-Pierre de Caussade wrote: *"The great and solid foundation of the spiritual life is to give oneself to God... in such a way that the good pleasure of God and his happiness... becomes our sole joy and good."*

The Joy of Loving Our Merciful God

There is a subtle form of joy in giving yourself to God. The joy of surrender is palpable. Doing God's will is something the saints enjoyed immensely.

St. Thérèse, who wanted to be especially pleasing to God, often said that the Lord is nothing but love, mercy and forgiveness. This appreciation of God's love gave her reason to rejoice. If you want to be especially pleasing to God, trust in His mercy. Mercy is another name for love as it confronts misery. Mercy is compassion, sensitivity and kindness.

In the third step of the 12 Step Program of Alcoholics Anonymous, members choose to turn their will over to God as they understand Him. We Christians understand Him as mercy personified.

The Scriptures abound in quotations about God's wonderful mercy. Because we are His children, He wants us to be merciful too. *"I want mercy, not sacrifice,"* says the Lord God. Those who are merciful become graceful carriers of Divine Love.

In the parable of the Good Samaritan, Jesus taught us how to be merciful. He asked this question: *"Who in your opinion was neighbor to the man who fell in among the robbers?" "The one who showed mercy,"* was the reply. *"And Jesus said: 'Go and do likewise'"* (Luke 10:37).

Being merciful is a great challenge. It doesn't take much imagination to see that the corporal and spiritual works of mercy are specific illustrations of mercy in action. If you were in need how would you want others to treat you? Here are the works of mercy.

The Seven Corporal Works of Mercy are:

1. Feeding the hungry;
2. Giving drink to the thirsty;
3. Clothing the naked;
4. Visiting the prisoners;
5. Sheltering the homeless;
6. Visiting the sick;
7. Burying the dead.

The Seven Spiritual Works of Mercy are:

1. Instructing the ignorant;
2. Counseling the doubtful;
3. Consoling the sorrowful;
4. Admonishing sinners;
5. Forgiving of injuries;
6. Bearing wrongs patiently;
7. Praying for the living and the dead.

Pray for the grace to be merciful.

Jesus said, *"Blessed are the merciful for they shall obtain mercy."* But never forget the sad truth that being merciful may cause you trouble. Many people do not want to forgive.

Jesus got Himself into deep trouble by being merciful. He always stood against the merciless. For instance, the legalistic spirit of the Pharisees led them to insist on the letter of the law. They came after Jesus with a vengeance for what they thought was His laxity in observing the law. Their venom eventually led to His crucifixion.

Mercy and perseverance are among the greatest virtues. Both require an abundance of love. Love endures all things. However, these virtues come at a high price.

Two of my favorite saints are St. Joan of Arc and St. Thomas More. They have much in common with Jesus. Both received the adulation of the people at one point in their lives, but later both were unjustly condemned to death.

Joan was called a witch, and Thomas was condemned as a traitor. Each could have changed the events leading to their execution by recanting. In France, Cauchon demanded that Joan save herself by admitting that she was possessed by an evil spirit. In England, King Henry VIII begged Thomas to sign the oath of supremacy in exchange for his life. He would not submit, even for his king.

Joan was bold with Cauchon: *"Time and again I have told you... all I have done was at God's command and He must be served first."* Thomas More refused to accede to Henry's plea, saying, *"I have to follow a higher authority than the king."*

Like Jesus, Joan and Thomas were courageous in their loyalty to their Father in heaven. Even though they were terrified by the threats made against them, they ultimately accepted their destiny as martyrs. Joan was tied to a stake and set afire. Thomas was publicly beheaded. Like Jesus, in their final moments, each of them begged God to be merciful to their persecutors.

Jesus, of course, is the model of all holiness. The saints are merely reflections of His holy Light. The lives of St. Joan of Arc and St. Thomas More are stunningly similar to the life of Jesus. Their fidelity to God's word, and the price they paid for that fidelity, became the stuff of legends.

What does this have to do with you and me? Does imitating Jesus mean that a Christian must be arrested and sentenced to death in order to demonstrate worthiness? No, but it does mean that all of us must be faithful to God's word no matter what the circumstances.

Jesus said, not everyone who says "Lord, Lord" will be saved, but only those who hear the word of God and act upon it. The importance of standing up for what is right at home, in school, at work, before the town council or anywhere, cannot be underestimated.

Jesus, The Source of All Holiness

Ultimately all holiness comes from Jesus Christ. He left us His Holy Spirit to inspire us to live bravely and joyfully because of the knowledge of His love. Jesus was considered absurd by the intellectuals of His day; others thought him to be a madman with a flair for attracting attention to Himself. But Jesus was not an ordinary man. He performed miracles; He rose from the dead, and to this day, He continues to live in His people. All who call Him Lord and Savior abide in His love. He heals and saves sinners, generation after generation.

New enemies arise every century to challenge His legacy and His teachings.

At the end of the nineteenth century, the Christian community had been badly battered by the rationalists and atheists. Immanuel Kant taught that man should recognize no authority superior to himself. To Kant, man's mind and will were supreme. He insisted that each person should create his own religion and morality.

Karl Marx, the father of Communism, rejected the idea of divine providence, saying that economics is in control of history, not God. He taught that a controlled, atheistic state was the answer to all human problems.

Nietzsche denounced religious faith as absurd. *"In Christianity neither morality, nor religion has even a single point of contact with reality... this is a world of pure fiction which falsifies, devalues and negates reality."*

In the world of literature, other voices scorned religious faith. Julian Huxley in England, Ernest Haeckel in Germany, Jean Paul Sartre in France – the theme was the same for each of them: Christian faith, at best, is a pious fancy and an enemy of all human progress.

Where has the worldly "wisdom" of these atheists and skeptics taken us? What has been the legacy of these enemies of Jesus Christ? History answers those questions for us: the Communist death camps, the death and extermination of millions in World War II, which was unleashed by Nietzsche's disciple, Adolf Hitler. He gave us the Holocaust and the destruction of Western Europe.

Those who are wise remain faithful to the Lord. He lives among us until the end of time. He alone is the hope of nations. He alone is the Author of all human progress.

We honor Jesus by exalting the cross. We also remember that Jesus said, *"I have told you all these things that your joy may be full."*

We revere the cross, not as an end in itself, but as the price paid for our redemption. Good Friday is one day in what the Liturgy of the Church calls "The Joyful Season of Lent." Easter Sunday, which proclaims the resurrection of Jesus Christ, is the highest holy day in the Christian calendar.

"We are an Easter people and Alleluia is our song," wrote St. Augustine. We cannot allow ourselves to become joyless creatures. There are plenty of reasons for feeling discouraged at times, but Christ told us to *"Take heart."* With a little effort we can aspire to joy. *"Ask and you will receive,"* says the Lord.

Christians tend to be about as joyful as they make up their minds to be. Too many give in to self-pity. One of the basic building blocks of joy is found in the will to bear discomfort.

A spirit of cheerful acquiescence in difficult circumstances is heroic, but not impossible. Think about this, your most pressing problems today will be forgotten ten years from now. Look at life from the perspective of eternity. Even if things are discouraging now, it will pass.

Knowing that God really loves you, that His power and strength are available to you, brings a glimmer of joy to the soul. Reject your negative thoughts. Commit the past to God's mercy, and the future to His loving providence. Live in the here and now, and claim the joy He intends for you.

Remember your union with God depends more on His love for you than it does on your love for Him. Do not be discouraged that you are weak and unworthy. No one is worthy of the infinite love that God lavishes on us. Never doubt His goodness.

Forgiveness is another name for love. Enjoy the gift of being forgiven.

The Difference Between Worry and Fear

There is such a thing as legitimate worry. Normal people worry about lots of things they have to do to make their lives productive and meaningful. Planning for any future event involves worry. Whether it's for a vacation, a wedding, a new job, or a trip to the dentist, worry is a normal part of living.

But there is a dark fear that is rooted in a failure to trust in God's unchanging love. Doubt and hopelessness can grow and become deadly enemies of the soul. If that kind of fear strikes you from time to time, turn it over to the Lord immediately. Use St. Teresa's prayer to get back to reality: *"Let nothing disturb you, let nothing cause you fear... whoever has the Lord needs nothing else, God alone suffices."* Learn to laugh at your fears. With a loving God, you really have nothing to fear, not even yourself. He is with you in all circumstances. The joy of loving God can become the dominant theme of your life.

Joy is the infallible sign of the presence of God. It may take you a little while to get your mind to accept this gift of God's Joyful Presence within you, but when you do, no matter what kind of a personality you have, your joy will be full. *"Rejoice in the Lord always! Again I say rejoice! The Lord is at hand. Have no anxiety about anything"* (Philippians 4:4).

This challenge has always intrigued me. Not only does Paul tell us not to worry about anything, he tells us to *"Rejoice always!"* It seems a bit farfetched, especially coming from Paul. Here was a man facing trial, and suffering bodily punishment. He was in prison awaiting a cruel execution. And yet he managed by the grace of God to put aside his natural fears.

What I find particularly interesting is that he makes a definite connection between the dismissal of anxiety and the presence of joy. He is not telling us to banish fear and then rejoice. What he is saying is that we should *"Rejoice in all circumstances, and have no anxiety about anything."* He puts the decision to rejoice at the top of the list, because he knows that joy, once chosen, liberates a person from anxiety. Freedom from fear will follow the will's decision to be joyful in all circumstances.

We may not be able to eliminate all feelings of fear by a simple act of the will, i.e., by merely saying "I will not be afraid," but we can control our thoughts. By choosing to be upbeat and hopeful we can block out the fear. The mind only has room for one set of ideas at a time. Choose joy!

By concentrating on God's love and protection, we are healed. When there is a joyful awareness of His presence, anxiety tends to dissolve. Once we center on the idea that Jesus died to free us from our fears, real spiritual progress begins.

Paul is telling us that the very act of rejoicing is in itself a kind of exorcism of fear. Anxiety cannot flourish in a joyful heart. Tranquilizers may help to quiet anxiety, but faith and joy dispel fear in a more permanent way. Faith in the reality of God's love brings a subtle joy to the soul. Rejoicing in the Lord is the work of the Holy Spirit.

"Be not anxious... Do not be afraid." Mother Teresa listened to Jesus and saw His face in everyone. She said Jesus often comes to us in "distressing disguises." She heard Jesus saying, as she approached those who were dying in the streets of Calcutta, *"What you do for the least of my brothers you do for me"* (Matthew 25:40).

Most of us are not holy enough to get beyond our fears. Jean Vanier was an exception. He dedicated his life to the care of mentally challenged adults, and once said: *"We are afraid of those in misery because they constitute a danger to us. Their poverty challenges our riches. So we raise barriers to keep them from sight."*

Fear is an enemy of love and the antithesis of joy. It causes discouragement and despair; it stirs up anger and resentment. Most of all it prevents a joyful heart from flourishing. The saints all experienced times of intense fear, but with the help of God they managed to overcome their fears. For this reason they are worthy of our honor and respect.

WHAT MAKES A SAINT A SAINT?

The last century has produced many saints. Some of them have already been proposed for canonization, others have not. In this book I will be presenting personal encounters and interviews that I have had with some of the saints who are now up for canonization, as well as a few others who will probably never be canonized, though all of them are among the holiest people of the twentieth century.

What actually makes a saint a saint?

St. Thérèse of Lisieux tried to answer that question, and here are her thoughts on the matter:

> *I wondered for a long time why God has preferences, why all souls don't receive an equal amount of graces.*
>
> *I was surprised when I saw Him shower His extraordinary favors on saints who had offended Him, for instance, Saint Paul and Saint Augustine, and whom He forced, so to speak, to accept His graces.*
>
> *When reading the lives of the saints, I was puzzled at seeing how our Lord was pleased to caress certain ones from the cradle to the grave, allowing no obstacle in their way when coming to Him, helping them with such favors that they were unable to soil the immaculate beauty of their baptismal robe.*

I wondered why poor savages died in great numbers without even having heard the name of God pronounced.

Jesus deigned to teach me this mystery. He set before me the book of nature; I understood how all the flowers He has created are beautiful, how the splendor of the rose and the whiteness of the lily do not take away the perfume of the little violet or the delightful simplicity of the daisy. I understood that if all flowers wanted to be roses, nature would lose her springtime beauty, and the fields would no longer be decked out with little wild flowers.

And so it is in the world of souls, Jesus' garden. He willed to create great souls comparable to lilies and roses, but He has also created smaller ones, and these must be content to be daisies or violets, destined to give joy to God's glances when He looks down at His feet. God does not call those who are worthy but those whom He pleases.

Holiness consists in doing His will; that is, in being what He wills us to be.

Jesus said, "*Learn of me for I am meek and humble of heart.*" Doing God's will makes people meek and humble of heart. Saints are saints:

Because they are cheerful when it is difficult to be cheerful;
Patient when it is hard to be patient;
Because they push forward when they want to stand still.
They keep silent when they want to talk; and
they are agreeable when they want to be disagreeable.
That's all. It is quite simple, and always will be.

St. Paul also had some comments on the subject when he spoke about love. Christian charity, another term for love, is the essence of Christian perfection.

"Love is patient, is kind,
love does not envy, is not pretentious,
is not self-seeking, is not provoked,
thinks no evil,
does not rejoice over wickedness
but rejoices with the truth;
bears with all things, believes all things,
hopes all things, endures all things"
(1 Corinthians 13:4-7).

The saints excelled in love. In fact they were outstanding in all three of the theological virtues: faith, hope and love. Most of us are not saints. We are more like "saints in training." We are capable of a real faith, but we are often weak in the virtue of hope, which leaves us vulnerable to the power of fear. Hope enables us to trust God in all circumstances.

Those who are weak in hope, allow their confidence to be undermined by fear and hesitation. They forget that they must learn to trust God. The saints knew the importance of the virtue of hope.

The word "hope" comes from the Latin "virtus" meaning "power." Hope is a gift which enables us to trust God in all circumstances. Without trust, the soul becomes beset with fear. When Jesus said, *"Be not afraid,"* He was commanding us to be brave by trusting in Him alone.

The saints were not afraid to do God's will, even if it put their life in danger. Each of them had the courage to follow their conscience in spite of opposition, and all of them managed to work against their fears in the cruel battles of life.

The center of the human personality is in the will. People often feel powerless and weak in their struggle to do God's will, but those with real faith, which leads to courage, are able to hope for the best. They know that *"with God all things are possible."*

If you want to be a saint, will it

The will has only one function: to say "yes" or "no." All kinds of thoughts flood the mind every day. Some are noble, but others are toxic. Saying yes to the noble thoughts, and no to the toxic ones is key to one's spiritual and emotional health.

Emotions soon express themselves in one's actions. A person who feels hurt and abused will become angry, and the anger, if left unchecked, can lead to violent actions.

The saints know that they have to control their thoughts in order to keep on an even keel. Jesus said that, in order to seek first the Kingdom of God, we must return good for evil, and turn the other cheek. The Holy Spirit gives us the grace to learn from Jesus, who was heroically brave against evildoers, but meek and humble of heart before God.

Cooperating with God's grace eventually comes down to the exercise of one's will. That's why St. Thomas Aquinas said, *"If you want to be a saint, will it."*

The will is a faculty of the soul, which must say "no" to toxic thinking. You must learn to dis-identify with any thoughts that are not from God.

Remember: **You are not your thoughts**.

No, you are the observer of your thoughts. You have the power to reject self-destructive thoughts, which are always uninvited intruders, like an invasion of mice in the living room. The best way to exterminate them is by nurturing good and holy thoughts.

Sometimes the enemy plants thoughts in our minds that lead to self-sabotage, and self-destruction. Jesus said, pay no attention to them, *"Be not afraid, for in this world you will have many troubles, but cheer up for I have overcome the world."*

To have peace of mind, you must have the courage to reject self-defeating thoughts and behavior.

The saints knew how to take control of their thoughts and emotions. They quickly rejected fear and self-pity. In reading my conversations with the saints of our past century, you will see how they fought off their fears, and overcame the opposition. They all obeyed the words of Jesus, and sought first the Kingdom of Heaven.

St. Teresa of Avila is an example of this kind of determination to cooperate with God's grace. Born near Avila, Spain, in 1515, she learned to reject all toxic self-defeating thoughts in her own way.

Somehow she knew that she had to trust in God, no matter what others might say about her efforts to reform the sisters of the Carmelite community.

Once she began thinking of herself as a reformer, called by God to do something special for God, she braced herself to take the heat when others opposed her. She rejected the idea of self-pity, and controlled her temptation to cry by writing a little prayer for herself. She repeated the following words constantly:

Let nothing disturb you,
Let nothing cause you fear.
God is unchanging.
Patience obtains all.
Whoever has God, needs nothing else.
God alone suffices.

This prayer became her mantra, and sustained her all through those long years of struggle and rejection. Eventually, her courage paid big dividends.

In 1562, after a long period of waiting for Rome's answer to her appeal, she obtained the approval of the Superior General of her Order to start a new community, which was to be called the Reformed Carmelites.

She had won the battle on all fronts. For years she had been accused of being too proud and stubborn, but she persevered, and won for herself a rich harvest of graces in the process. By going against her fears and self-doubt God helped her to bring about widespread reform in the lives of religious women everywhere.

When you choose God's will rather than your own toxic thoughts, your emotions will follow suit, and you will begin to live a purposeful life, and move beyond mediocrity.

Cooperation with God's grace is the goal of every saint. Let me share with you my experiences with some of the holy people of the last century.

ENCOUNTERS WITH HOLINESS

HOPE

Hope looks for the good in people instead of
harping on the worst.

Hope opens doors where despair closes them.

Hope discovers what can be done instead of
grumbling about what cannot.

Hope draws its power from a deep trust in God
and the basic goodness of mankind.

Hope "lights a candle" instead of "cursing the darkness."

Hope regards problems, small or large, as opportunities.

Hope cherishes no illusions, nor does it yield to cynicism.

Hope sets big goals and is not frustrated by
repeated difficulties or setbacks.

Hope pushes ahead when it would be easy to quit.

Hope puts up with modest gains,
realizing that the "longest journey starts with one step."

Hope accepts misunderstandings as the price for
serving the greater good of others.

Hope is a good loser because it has the divine
assurance of final victory.

Father James Keller

1

FATHER JAMES KELLER

We at The Christophers are simply applying to the heart of America the same simple approach used by a Maryknoll missionary who brings Christ into a pagan city in China. Instead of sitting in the outskirts of the city, complaining or criticizing, he goes in – as Christ said to do – and puts into literal effect an old Chinese proverb: "It is better to light one candle than to curse the darkness"; even if only one missioner goes into the city, it is better than none at all. Even if a missionary makes no apparent progress, or is persecuted and imprisoned, nevertheless he is there.

Father James Keller was a spiritual father to millions of loyal followers. He was a holy priest, a visionary, and a skilled communicator. Born in 1900, the son of James Keller and Margaret Selby, he was the fourth of six children. The family lived in Oakland, California, which was probably why the newly ordained Father Keller was made the West Coast vocation director and fund-raiser for the Maryknoll Fathers, a missionary society with headquarters in New York.

He was ordained on August 15, 1925, and dreamed of doing missionary work in China. However, the Maryknoll Fathers had other ideas. They decided to keep him in the States doing promotional work for Maryknoll. He was deeply disappointed. Nevertheless, the obedient priest, after a few years of working on the West Coast, made some Hollywood connections, and this experience opened the door to a future he never dreamed possible.

He began to see how he could use the mass media to spread his missionary vision to people everywhere. At first he invited celebrities in the movie industry to help him spread his message of hope. They were only too happy to oblige because this was a time when many baseless accusations of anti-Americanism were bandied around. Keller was viewed as a super-patriot, so the entertainment community sought to be associated with him. It was a badge of honor to be in his films and TV tapings.

He saw his Gospel mission as one of promoting Christ, as well as good government and patriotism. The growing threat of atheistic Communism led men like Senator Joseph McCarthy to go on a witch-hunt. Father Keller wanted no part of negativism. He always stressed the need for positive, constructive action in solving our national problems, and in bringing Gospel values to the mainstream of life.

He decided to ask for permission to start a brand new organization to teach people to become Christ-bearers. At first Maryknoll's board was hesitant, but gradually they came around and allowed him to launch out with his grand plan of using the mass media to help make this a better world.

Bishop James A. Walsh, a Maryknoll bishop, always stressed the idea that every individual missionary was another Christ. The word *Christopher*, which Keller took as the name of his new venture, came from the Greek word, *"christo-phoros,"* meaning Christ-bearer.

Fr. Keller came into real prominence after the Second World War.

The Cold War was intensifying, and the times were filled with intrigue. As the threat of nuclear devastation loomed on

4

the horizon, Father Keller spoke out against Communism, challenging people of all faiths, and people of no particular faith, to work together to help make this a better world.

He knew that we needed spiritual answers as well as political ones in the ideological battle for the minds and hearts of people. In order to prevent the atheistic philosophy of the Soviet Union from spreading, Keller motivated his followers to choose meaningful careers, where their gifts and talents could do the most good: careers in politics, education, and communications. He taught people to promote the common good by using their gifts and talents in the service of others. It was the Gospel message adapted to the times. His was a prophetic voice.

We rarely recognize the saints among us until after they're gone. We seem to understand them better in the light of their spiritual legacy. Pope Benedict XVI, in an interview with *Giorni*, an Italian newspaper, shortly after he was elected said, "*There are many more saints than is possible to canonize.*" That is certainly true in the case of Father Keller. Millions of people have been touched by his dedication and vision. He believed that the gifts we receive at birth are God's gifts to us; and what we do with them is our gift to God.

Keller also believed that by working together, people of all faiths can change this world for the better. His vision caught my attention in 1949, two months before my graduation from high school, when my Dad gave me a red covered book and said, "*I want you to read this; I think you'll like it.*" The book was Father Keller's best-seller, *You Can Change the World*. I not only read it, but I loved it.

I was young, idealistic and confused about my future. I knew I wanted to do something meaningful with my life, and Father Keller's book gave me the clarity and optimism I needed. I came to see that I had a God-given mission to do something in this world that would change it for the better. I didn't know what it would be, but I knew it was just a question of time before I'd find it.

After high school, I went to study for a degree in business administration at Fordham University. I soon realized that conducting business was not what I really wanted to do with my life. I wanted to move in a different direction. Father Keller gave me the courage to think outside of the box, and I found myself considering a career in television.

I had to work my way through college anyway, so I decided to apply for a job as a page at NBC Studios in New York City. I got the job and worked from 5:00 p.m. to midnight on the big NBC shows starring Sid Caesar, Perry Como, Robert Montgomery, and many others. It was all quite exciting, at first, but gradually I became disillusioned. All the glamour seemed to be so unreal to me.

My interests began moving in a more serious direction. After college the Korean War was coming to an end, but the draft was still in effect. I was drafted and had to spend two years in the Army, one year as a Military Policeman, and in the second year the Chaplain asked me to be his assistant. I enjoyed that year very much, and when my time was up, and I was discharged, I knew I wanted to be a priest.

I entered the seminary, and was ordained for the Diocese of Paterson on May 28, 1960. I'm telling you all this because it has a bearing on my connection to Father Keller.

After ordination, the bishop sent me to Catholic University in Washington, D.C., to get a degree in Canon Law. I didn't want to study Canon Law, but in those days you had no choice; you just did what you were told. Once I got my doctorate, I returned and the bishop assigned me to work part-time in a parish, and part-time in the Marriage Tribunal, which is the office dealing with marriage annulments among other things.

Eventually I was put in charge of the Tribunal with the title of judicial Vicar to the bishop. I served in that capacity for the next ten years. In 1970 the priests of the diocese elected me their clergy personnel representative. I did this for five years, and was even elected to be president of the National Association of Church Personnel Administrators. I think the fact that I had a national position put me in contention to be Father Keller's successor.

After a long and debilitating battle with Parkinson's disease, Father Keller died on February 7, 1977. His assistant, Father Richard Armstrong, who had worked by his side for over twelve years, was placed in charge. I never met Armstrong, but a few months after the loss of their founder, he called me to get some canonical advice.

After we finished talking about his situation, he told me that he would be resigning and that The Christophers were searching for a new director. I presumed that his replacement would be a Maryknoll priest, but to my surprise he said no. Maryknoll decided not to fill the vacancy since they wanted to stay focused on the foreign missions. Therefore, finding a new director was now the task of The Christophers board of directors, not the Maryknoll board.

My heart leaped at the mere possibility of being a candidate for the job. I hesitantly told Dick about my admiration for Fr. Keller, and my early dream of working in the field of television. Without a moment of hesitation, he encouraged me to apply for the job.

Thinking that I was not sufficiently qualified, I did nothing for three weeks, but the idea tormented me. Finally I realized that I'd have nothing to lose by applying. So I wrote to the search committee, and told them I was interested. A series of interviews followed. The suspense lasted for nine months. In the meantime, my bishop, Lawrence Casey, died. My heart sank because I knew that even if The Christophers wanted me, I wouldn't be available. An acting administrator doesn't have the power to release a priest for an assignment outside of the diocese during a vacancy in the episcopal office. I simply presumed that it was all over for me.

However, after months of waiting, the unexpected happened. On February 27, 1978, almost a year to the day of Father Keller's death, a board member, Father Ron Saucci, M.M., called to tell me that they had chosen me to be the successor of Father Keller. I almost fainted. The timing was amazing. That very same week Msgr. Frank J. Rodimer was named the new Bishop of Paterson, N.J. He was a friend, and it didn't take me long to ask for his permission to accept the position. The new bishop said yes immediately. I couldn't believe my good fortune.

In the publicity release about my appointment, I expressed my sincere thanks to Bishop Rodimer, The Christopher Board, my family, and in a special way to the Maryknoll Fathers for their wonderful support of my appointment. I have always respected the close connection between The Christophers and the Maryknoll Fathers, who enabled Father Keller to create this new organization.

The Christophers can be described as a mass media organization with two main divisions: one, a TV and radio production company, and the other, a print media publishing house. Today the organization is running under the leadership of a lay man, Dennis Heaney, who was once the president of the Catholic Press Association of the United States and Canada, and who also served as a former editor of two Catholic newspapers, *The Tidings* in Los Angeles, and *The Catholic Spirit* in St. Paul, Minnesota.

Father Keller's spirit is still very much alive today at The Christophers. Here are some of my favorite quotes from him:

> *Strive to be motivated by a consuming desire to bring the love and truth of Christ to all mankind to right the wrongs that the Communists exploit – no study, work or sacrifice will be too great for you... It has become habitual and perhaps fashionable to disdain government as something beneath us. Today*

*the chief obstacle to good government is the widespread belief
that it is a job for someone else, not for us.*

One of his most popular books, *Good Government is Your
Business*, has chapter headings, which proclaim Fr. Keller's pa-
triotic message:

*It's Your Country, Too!
Everyone Can Do Something
Politics Affects You Whether You Realize It or Not
The Beginnings of Government
City Government Depends on You
State Government Vitally Affects You
It's Your National Government
What Everybody Should Know about Civil Service
The Source of American Strength*

The book sold over 300,000 copies. One reader wrote to
say, "I firmly believe this book changed my life. It gave me the
insight that the road of the 'individual' working alone to do good
is not an easy road. This book gave me the confidence to hold my
ground when the going got rough."

Obviously Father Keller struck a chord in the heart of
America in a way no other Catholic priest had ever done. He
was not a rabble-rouser, or a political activist; he was essentially
a missionary who saw America as mission territory. Here is how
he explained his vision:

*As true followers of Christ, we have a fourfold obligation:
1. to those who are members of the Catholic Church;
2. to those who are interested in entering the Church;
3. to those who have no desire to become Catholic;
4. to those who hate the Church and fight against it.*

Father Keller added,

Most Catholics show a laudable interest in the first two groups. But much remains to be done in regard to the other two... If we succeed in nothing more than getting them to be one degree more disposed towards Christ, to offer one prayer or do one small deed for the love of God, it is an important step in the right direction. The least act on their part may open the way to the greater graces they need so much...

His focus was geared to the words and deeds of Jesus.

Our Lord used weddings, dinners, parties and many types of worldly occasions as well as persons, both good and bad, to remind men of their spiritual destiny... Combining informal and dignified entertainment with a Christopher message is a most effective way to emphasize individual responsibility and initiative in restoring God's order to the world.

Father Keller urged people to get into the media so that they could bring to it a positive contribution for the common good. *"The big need,"* he said, *"is to encourage people with good ideas to go into the marketplace rather than to concentrate too much on driving out those with evil design."*

He stood above the liberal-conservative Catholic debate His only concern was in doing missionary work. His thoughts remained spiritually lofty.

Every human being, regardless of creed or color, is made to the image and likeness of God and possesses a soul more precious than all the world and has only one purpose here: to prepare his soul for eternity by knowing, loving, and serving his Maker in this life. To help each and every soul,

God sent His Divine Son to redeem us and give us both a plan, and unlimited assistance to attain eternal salvation. We have already received the gift of faith but nearly two-thirds of mankind has not. God has left it in our hands to see that they do.

These words still inspire me to be a carrier of Christ.

HE WENT ON

Jesus from His childhood had the deadliest of enemies,
yet He went on.
Jesus had the very worst interpretations put upon His kindest actions,
yet He went on.
Jesus had all His words falsely reported and twisted,
yet He went on.
Jesus was criticized and condemned as one who was unorthodox,
yet He went on.
Jesus was sneered at by the great and patronized by the learned,
yet He went on.
Jesus knew very little gratitude, He was slighted, and scorned,
yet He went on.
Jesus was deserted by everyone, even His best friends,
yet He went on.
Jesus was betrayed with a kiss, by one He had most trusted,
yet He went on.
Jesus was denied by Peter, the one on whom He most relied,
yet He went on.
Jesus was nailed to a cross as a criminal between two other criminals,
yet He went on.
Jesus was never without those who hated Him,
who plotted against Him, who maligned Him behind His back,
and He knew they would succeed,
yet He went on.
Jesus is passed over and condemned generation after generation,
Yet He goes on.

Archbishop Goodier, S.J.

2

FATHER WALTER CISZEK, S.J.

*When I was arrested as a spy, I was brainwashed for 5 years
in Lubiyanka Prison. Daily interrogations were done to
break me down. Instead of going along with them I refused
and was eventually sent to the Arctic Circle. And this was
by mistake. I was supposed to be with what they called the
political prisoners. And instead of sending me with the
political prisoners I was sent with the criminals.*

In 1939 a newly-ordained American priest, Walter Ciszek, S.J., was
captured by the Russian army in Poland. When war broke out
between Russia and Germany, the Russians accused him of being
a spy for the Vatican, and sent him to Moscow's notorious Lubiyanka Prison where he served 5 years of solitary confinement. He
was later sentenced to 15 years of hard labor in the Siberian slave
camps located inside the Arctic Circle. While imprisoned in the
freezing cold, he kept the word of God alive in his heart.

Father Walter was all but given up for dead by friends and
family, but to everyone's amazement, in 1963, with the help of
the U.S. Attorney General Robert F. Kennedy, he was returned
to the United States in exchange for two Soviet spies.

Despite his long exile in that living hell, Father Ciszek
returned to have many good years of ministry at the Russian

Center of Fordham University. It was there that I met him, after reading the two books he wrote about his experiences: *With God in Russia* and *He Leadeth Me*. I went to visit with him many times, and enjoyed talking with him. I found him to be a modest man, and a holy priest with sparkling blue eyes.

He once wrote these precious words: *"Nothing can trouble a soul that accepts every moment of every day as a gift from the hand of God."* There were so many crushing days in his captivity that I wondered how he was able to survive and reach such a beautiful state of peace.

In an interview I did with him for The Christophers, I asked Father Ciszek if the memories of those prison days still haunt him. He was a little flustered by the lights and cameras at HBO Studios in New York City where we did the taping, but the richness of his soul came through beautifully.

WC: Well, reflecting on some of the things that happened to me and contrasting to it what I have now, it is very encouraging and I'd say very revealing in this sense that it has given me a deeper insight to what life is, and what the life to come is. It is all very encouraging. What happened in the plan of God has given me something that I never had in my life. It's a growth process, we are moving to a goal that we are attaining. We're destined for something great, we are participating and sharing it all the time with other people. You can be God's instruments not only in words but also in the way you behave and what you are.

JC: Tell me about your early life.

WC: I was born stubborn. I was also tough, not in the polite sense of the word, but in the sense in which our neighbors used that word in Shenandoah, Pennsylvania where I grew up. They shook their heads and called me "tough." This is nothing to be proud of, but it shows as honestly as I know how to state it, what sort of raw material God had to work with.

I was a bully, a leader of a gang, a street fighter, and most of the fights I picked on purpose, just for devilment. I had no use for school except insofar as it had a playground where I could fight or wrestle... Things were so bad in fact that while I was still in grammar school, my father actually took me to the police station insisting that they send me to reform school.

And yet my father was the kindest of men. He was simply at his wits end. Talking to me did no good. Thrashing me only gave me an opportunity to show how tough I was.

JC: Years later, in Russia, you were in jail with common criminals. How did your raw personality help you to deal with those prisoners?

WC: When I was with the criminals I felt at one with these people. Not that I was prepared to change my life and go that way, but because I'd say, for a deeper reason. And the deeper reason was the training I got in the spiritual life. Remember the purpose that I had in coming to Russia was to touch lives and bring Christ to those who did not know him.

It was my purpose and I was permeated with that idea. When I met the reality of prison life, when I came there, I felt the impossibility of giving what I had to give. I had to slow down and take things as they developed. This is why I got involved in an entirely new apostolate. It was so interesting and it required all the energies of my whole being, I'd say to the point of exhaustion.

JC: May I ask a question before you go further with that? We mentioned at the opening of the program that you were arrested for being a Vatican spy. Were you? Did you have anything to do with the Vatican?

WC: Not directly, never.

JC: How about indirectly?

WC: Indirectly I got permission from the Holy See, through my bishop and through my superior, to go to Poland as a missionary. That's why I went over there. I didn't go on my own. I just went to be a priest.

JC: In other words the spy charge was bogus. But what exactly did you get permission for?

WC: To be a priest.

JC: To be a priest?

WC: Yes, I went over there to be a priest and to learn about this new system called Communism. I was doing that as a worker in order to support myself. Then, when I was arrested as a spy, I was brainwashed for five years in Lubiyanka Prison. Daily interrogations were done to break me down. Instead of going along with them I refused and was eventually sent to the Arctic Circle. And this was by mistake. I was supposed to be with what they called the political prisoners. And instead of sending me with the political prisoners I was sent with the common criminals who were rejected in society. And I saw these people for the first time in my life, and that they were just like other people. I learned that these miserable creatures were from families that were broken. They didn't know their own fathers. They always had some kind of adverse feeling towards authority because they were raised in foster homes, they were put in houses where they never had the protection of a real mother or any real relative. Because of this they developed a kind of antagonism, an uncontrolled passion of anger.

And this is what I came in contact with, yet their condition was a human thing that could be corrected. It's always possible to correct such personality flaws in human nature. And this is what I worked for. I'd get to know these people, and it was then for the first time that I saw what my mission or my apostolate was. It wasn't to those that didn't need me, those who had religion and all; it was to these people that had no concept of what religion was. They were in an atheistic country and were educated in that way.

JC: Were you just a worker to them, part of the slave labor force? Did they know you were a priest?

WC: They didn't really know it, and this is what baffles me today, and it baffled me before. I never went to people to convert them or to instruct them on religion. But they always came to me. I said I was just as miserable as they were. I was just as degraded by the system. The clothes I wore; the exhaustion that I felt; the tiredness of the work; the hunger, was just the same. The temptation was always there to commit some crime just to get some food, or to escape, to get liberated from what I was suffering there, what I was experiencing at that time. And yet in all that I felt that the other element, the modifying element in me, my conscience would say what you're here for, that you're supposed to be a witness of something deeper. That tension kind of balanced my life with them. Here for the first time I realized that I had to be a loving presence. Coming in contact with harsh reality and responding to it with a certain amount of love, compassion.

JC: How would you describe your main mission among them?

WC: To be a witness. I felt that for the first time. It wasn't to convert these people, because there's another part that would convert them. But to be what I was supposed to be, just to profess my religion, not to try theologically to prove anything, but in every situation react as best as I could with my convictions. I was aware of my failings, and human insufficiencies, of not being a full witness, yes that feeling was always there, but there was something else that made up for it, my powers were supplemented by the power of God in me and it was that which affected these people.

JC: I'm fascinated that you felt that your mission was simply to be present and return good for evil. Were there any other priestly functions that you did for the people in Siberia?

WC: Oh yes, but first of all let me explain something. When bad things happen to them they would get very angry, they'd rebel. They would curse the guards, curse other people, but I never did that. Not that I didn't feel the same emotional reactions, but I'd say by the power of God that was in me, I never lost control. I depended on the providence of God, and the power of God in me. And somehow I was effective in touching their souls. They were attracted and they asked me to tell them or teach them why do I behave like that. They thought I was doing some magic that I had some kind of a talisman or something. They wondered why I didn't fight back, why I didn't condemn the things that they condemned.

And I began explaining it was only by prayer that I could be this way, and to pray, I said, is the secret of dealing with a lot of life's problems. I'd tell them, here's where you have to begin, and I'd instruct them along, telling them about prayer and about sin. They didn't understand what sin is.

JC: Let's go back to prayer. You said you gave them a way to pray, and you gave them something to do. What was that?

WC: I told them that my secret was the Jesus Prayer, "Lord, Jesus have mercy upon me sinner." That was the whole prayer. And I told them if they want to live a happy life, if they want to conquer the difficulties in life, then say that prayer three times in the morning, three at noon and six times in the evening. That was it.

JC: How did they respond?

WC: Well, I would say in many ways. First of all by their hospitality. They would share things with me. And in the camp if you would share a piece of bread with a friend of yours that meant you respected him. That meant you're giving part of your life away.

But I on my side would never turn them away, when they came to tell me their difficulties or tell me their problems. I'd listen. Instead of having a little rest I'd have to listen to them, but I never refused and I wouldn't refuse now.

JC: Can you remember an example of helping someone?

WC: Yes. There is a certain kind of intuitive feeling people have, innate, and a lot of people have it. A woman came to me once, she said we don't have people like you here. And I said why? I work, I eat, I'm happy with you, I drink with you and everything. And she said but there's something in you, and especially this is the one thing she noticed, the young girls would come to me, and they would go with you any place.

But they would not go with Ivan, or some other man. And I asked why is that? We trust you she said. This is what I wanted to mention right in the beginning. That they gave me their confidence, their trust. And with God's help, I'm telling you, you can have people trusting you, it's not that I am affecting them, it is not because of me, but because of God's grace. They trusted me, and once that trust was established they let themselves be open to further teaching.

JC: Could I go back to a point that I found interesting. I'm not sure I heard the answer. When these prisoners, these are hardened criminals who were full of anger, came to you and found it unusual that you had a placid nature, and were forgiving toward the jailers, and they asked how you did it, how did you answer them? And how did you manage to keep your cool in the first place?

WC: First of all, I learned about prayer when I joined the Jesuits. My attraction to the Jesuits was not primarily to get an education. If I joined the Jesuits to be an educated man it sure turned out differently. (LAUGHTER)

I am different entirely from any scholar. But I was very much attracted by prayer, by the spiritual life. When I went to Theology in the Gregorian University I never could accept the lectures that they gave when they told of the rational approach to God. I saw beyond that and I wondered why don't they mention something about that deeper level. I was inexperienced in prayer, and they were only giving me an academic approach. So I had to take it on myself to do it. You asked me how did I develop the skill to keep my cool? I simply began to get more involved in prayer.

The Spiritual Exercises of St. Ignatius enticed me so much that I spent all the time I had, all my free time, developing it. When I went to the Soviet Union for those 24 years I never had a spiritual book to work from. It was all in my head. My memory developed so much in regard to the Spiritual Exercises that I could recall the Scriptures almost word for word by following the Spiritual Exercises. And that's what I did for 24 years. But something deeper happened to me along the way.

JC: What was that?

WC: I mention it in my book. It was a kind of watershed moment for me. I realized that in spite of all my suffering, I was still not abandoned to Divine Providence.

JC: I'd like to read that section from your book, *He Leadeth Me*, and then ask you to comment on it:

Slowly, reluctantly, under the gentle prodding of grace, I faced the truth that was at the root of my problem and my shame. The answer was a single word: "I". I was ashamed because I knew in my heart I had tried to do too much, and I failed. I felt guilty because I realized finally that I had asked for God's help, but had really believed in my own ability to avoid evil and to meet every challenge. I had spent much time in prayer over the years. I had come to appreciate and thank God for His Providence and care of me and of all men, but I never really abandoned myself to it... In short, I felt guilty and ashamed because in the last analysis I had relied almost completely on myself in this most critical test, and I had failed.

WC: Yes, it was a great humiliation to have tried so hard, only to realize that I wasn't doing it right. All prayer is good, and it gave me the strength to carry on all through the years, but there comes a time when we have to drop all that smacks of self, and rely on God in a new way.

JC: Can you tell me more about abandonment to Divine Providence? How does it work?

WC: When I first discovered the importance of abandonment, I didn't know whether I was making any progress or not. When I tried to move more deeply into a state of abandonment, I had the feeling that I was not doing it right, that this was not it. So I'd ask the Lord, *What do I do? How do I do it?*

You don't make much progress at first because you keep coming back to self; but you know you're in a new area. You aren't affected as much by your own failure as you used to be. You grow away from some of the ideas you had about proving yourself, about human courage, and things like that.

What you were before isn't eliminated, it keeps coming back, but a steady growing takes place, a new consciousness of God's control over you, a new attitude toward things as they happen. Temptations don't hit you quite the same way. You learn grace isn't only in the good things, but in the bad things as well. The misuse of grace is the mistake we make. We forget that God brings good out of everything.

JC: What did you mean when you said, you don't worry as much about succeeding?

WC: You begin to realize that whether you succeed or not is God's business. You get a freer perspective on your life. God is teaching you all the time about what you are and what you are not, to help you really live the life of abandonment. You learn that what you do or do not do in your spiritual program doesn't matter so much; what matters is the spirit in which you are working at the time.

I see God in me asking me to say Mass. You have to be convinced in faith that God is asking you to do it. This gives you trust, and if everything else fails, trust will save you.

JC: When it comes to abandonment to God, you're saying that trust is key. How does this actually work in practice?

WC: I think of my role as that of a sunken bucket... on the bottom of the sea, very deep, no movement, no bubbles. I sink myself into God like that. He has complete access to me. He is the One that moves me. He does everything; I do nothing.

JC: I wish I had time to pursue that a bit more, but I would like to ask a few more questions on a slightly different topic. Dostoyevsky once said that Russians are half saints and half savages. You seem to feel a bond with the Russian people. Can you talk a little about that comment?

WC: It's true, but not just of the Russians. For example, we all have the devil in us at times, but we don't let him take over. We have strong reactions of anger, bitterness, of hate and jealousy, but that isn't you; you may be affected that way, but when you are a man of prayer, you realize that that direction is not the answer to the real needs in life. Those feelings and inclinations can bring a great distortion to your life.

Like anger, I mean if it's not a righteous anger prompted by some injustice, it is likely to be a kind of madness that becomes a sin. But if you get that feeling of anger and use it properly you can use it as a power; as a good power. You can harness it and then you can get good work following out of it. It's an energy. It's that same energy of the will, which can either put you in the right direction or in the wrong direction. That means you can follow it because it's a good power; the will has added power, it can act; it's all in the will. The average person is not trained for that.

You see we were trained in the seminary. We had the insights of years and years of people who studied spirituality and they left this all to us in books, in examples, and we've been affected, we in the Church are very blessed. Many people didn't have that, so when bad things happen to them, they just blast right out in anger, going to extremes.

Then when they get it out of their system and the anger subsides, when it all cools down, they begin to show their true nature. And they are as good as they were before, before the anger came.

JC: I'd like to go back and reconstruct your average day during that period in Siberia. You were first arrested as a Vatican spy, and they sent you to Moscow's Lubiyanka Prison for five years of relentless interrogations. Then you were sentenced to 15 years at hard labor in Siberia. When you did your sentence, they released you, but you still had to remain in that region living among the people there. You said the natives would invite you to their homes. Tell us more about that time.

WC: Yes, it was in the Arctic Circle. But after I finished the 15 years of my sentence, I was released and had what I call semi-freedom. I had to report to the police every month and report what I was doing, and what I intended to do.

JC: During that period were you offering Mass? Did they question you on that kind of activity? I understand that they objected to it, and threatened you with further imprisonment if you didn't stop. What did you say to them in your own defense?

WC: Well, I said to them that I never go to these people's homes. They come to me. And if they ask me for a favor whether it's religion, whether it's confession, whether it's to say Mass, I said, I'm doing it as a favor; and your constitution has nothing to do with that. It's the human thing to do. And they would say to me that the written law is one thing, but you've lived here in the Soviet Union long enough to know there is unwritten law, and you better reflect and think about this.

JC: What did you do then?

WC: It didn't bother me. I just did what seemed right to me, and they never pressed me further on that. It was all part of a process of purification.

JC: What do you mean?

WC: Well, I don't care who you are, or what you did in life, the time comes when you have to change. You have to modify your life. Life experiences would show the direction you should take. I don't care how hard a man might be in his evil ways, there is something in him that is counterbalancing it all. There is always the invitation to balance your life. That's the great interior struggle we all share.

JC: If a person came to you and said I've suffered a great loss, I've been unjustly treated, how could God let this happen to me? What would you say?

WC: Well, I'd listen to him and say well this is the way you're affected now. I'd say, I'll pray for you. (I wouldn't tell him to pray because he's not ready to pray). I'd say that this is your present reaction but try to be open to whatever comes to you later, when you calm down, when you see things in a little different way. You will modify your decisions, and perhaps take different steps. There is a gentle way to deal with it. There is in us what we call grace, which comes from the power of God.

JC: What sustains you right now?

WC: I believe in heaven. I don't want to go to hell. (LAUGHTER) And I'm doing what I can. That's the whole thing. I pray. I try never to hurt anyone or anything. Not that I wouldn't like to blast out sometimes when I get angry, but that's not really me. That's more me when I'm off base. Then I go and do my little duties. If you're young you go running around. I did all that before. Now all I can do is have a deep faith. No matter what happens the Lord will see me through. I feel that it is the most effective way to live. I'm helping humanity in the process because of my true faith.

JC: The Lord is leading you.

WC: That's the whole thing.

JC: Thank you so much Father Ciszek for sharing your thoughts, and your life with us.

Father Ciszek is now being considered for canonization. For me his holiness and childlike simplicity made him a saint years ago, but he never knew it.

The saints represent the shining path,
which God Himself has traced throughout history.
Saints are the world's true reformers,
who have taught Christians that it is love, not ideologies,
which will save the world.

Pope Benedict XVI

3

DOROTHY DAY

I think fear is one of the most dangerous things; to get over one's fears and to teach your children to get over fears is very hard. Fear causes you to criticize a lot, you end up with a chip on your shoulder. You strike out in retaliation, and you end up getting hurt yourself; and partly it's your own fault... Children suffer much from fear but we can help relieve their anxiety – after all they have a guardian angel. I think we need to stress that fact and also have some faith that there is protection.

Dorothy always believed that fear is the tool of the devil. "Fear tells us to run away," she would say, "and forget all about the pursuit of holiness." But Jesus said, *"Be not afraid... ask and you shall receive, seek and you will find, knock and it shall be opened unto you."*

Dorothy Day always believed in the possibility of holiness. From the time of her conversion to the Catholic Church, she carried this message to the world. Many people regard Dorothy Day as a great American saint. After her death, Terence Cardinal Cooke of the Archdiocese of New York introduced her cause for canonization.

She was born in 1897 in Brooklyn Heights, New York City, the third child of Christian parents who did not practice their faith, and was baptized into her mother's Episcopal faith when she was twelve. She was not religiously involved as a teen, but became an inveterate reader of the social writings of anarchists and revolutionaries. She joined the Socialist Party in order to actively work for a change in society, which was plagued by poverty and unemployment during the Great Depression. In 1924, after two failed relationships, she fell in love with Forster Batterham, a biologist and anarchist, and lived in a common-law marriage with him. Tamar Teresa was born to them in March of 1926, and the wonder of this new life made her so happy it brought about a complete conversion to God, "No human creature could receive or contain so vast a flood of love and joy as I felt after the birth of my child." With this came her dramatic conversion to the faith. "The need to worship, to adore flooded my spirit... Through Tamar I came to know God."

Dorothy had Tamar baptized, and became a Catholic herself in December of 1927, a decision which ended her relationship with Batterham, who was an atheist. After that she devoted herself to a life of service to the poor.

On May 1, 1933 Dorothy Day and Peter Maurin co-founded the Catholic Worker movement in New York City. The newspaper by the same name was published in that first year. Her life of voluntary poverty, her direct action on behalf of the poor, and her absolute stance on nonviolence and pacifism have won the admiration, and in some cases the scorn, of millions of Americans. Christians of all denominations, and even non-Christians have been inspired by her life.

In November of 1972 *America* magazine devoted an entire issue to her, and the editors commented: "By now, if one had to choose a single individual to symbolize the best in the aspiration and actions of the American Catholic community during the last forty years, that one person would certainly be Dorothy Day. She edited and contributed articles to the *Catholic Worker* newspaper for nearly half a century."

Dorothy was one of God's brave and holy saints. She was an advocate of non-violence all her life. In the spirit of Jesus who said, "Learn of me for I am meek and gentle of heart," she learned to love the poor, the downtrodden, and the weak, and was never threatened by them.

Most people are afraid of poor people. Even those who want to help the poor, only do so through charitable donations, so as not to run the risk of being too close to them. Dorothy had no fear of the poor; in fact she loved them.

Before I present the interview I did with Dorothy, I'd like to tell you how I came to meet her. My friend, Father James McCoy, introduced me to her in 1951. He taught a course in religion at the Fordham University School of Business where I attended from 1949 to 1953. Though he was a priest of no particular importance, and will never be canonized, he was a saint to me, not only because he gave me his time, and patiently listened to my sophomoric faith problems, but because he was such an exemplary human being. He was my spiritual mentor for well over thirty years. I owe him more than words can express.

After I graduated from college I still had no serious thoughts about becoming a priest, but I was intrigued by Fr. McCoy's humility and holiness. Jim was also an independent thinker, and his ideas had a powerful impact on me, and my priesthood in later years.

He often said, *"Always act according to your convictions."* This kind of thinking endeared him to Dorothy Day, who often came to him for advice.

Jim was a man of tremendous strength and determination. He could care less about who agreed with him or not. I kept in touch with him over the years because he fascinated me, and gave me encouragement to follow my grace, wherever it would lead me. He answered so many of my questions, and was a pillar of strength for me when I was floundering in college.

When he was living in New York City, in the Jesuit community connected to Xavier High School, Dorothy Day came to him for confession, and from time to time would ask him to give a talk to the people at the Catholic Worker headquarters near the Bowery. Dorothy loved him because he was so much at home with the poor and downtrodden.

At this time, my plan was to pursue a career in TV production. I wanted to be rich, and have a great family, but the thought of being a priest kept pestering my conscience. Dorothy Day's life challenged me; her idealism made me think more deeply about what I was going to do with my life.

Actually it was Jim McCoy's example that guided me toward the priesthood, but he never once suggested that I think about becoming a priest. He would brush off my attempts to discuss it with him, saying that such matters were between God and me alone. He never wanted to interfere with my freedom. In fact, he suggested that it was possible that I was mistaking a vocation to holiness for a vocation to the priesthood. At the time, I really didn't want to trot off to a seminary, so the thought that I had a vocation to holiness, and not to the priesthood was a relief of sorts.

Jim said we are all called to holiness, so I figured at least I could deal with that. I put the idea of the priesthood aside once and for all, or so I thought.

After graduation in 1953, I was drafted into the Army. The Korean War was not yet over, and after sixteen weeks of basic training I ended up in Fort Sam Houston, Texas as a Military Policeman. In the service I began thinking more seriously about the priesthood, and by the time I was discharged, I had finally decided to be a priest, if God would have me. I wrote to tell Fr. Jim, and he replied, *"Good for you. I wanted it to be entirely your decision so that later in life you would never be tempted to believe that anyone put pressure on you."*

I appreciated that. Jim could relate easily with everyone, and he respected their freedom. He dealt with people in high society with the same ease he mingled with drug addicts and derelicts. Without putting on any airs, he was a priest's priest. He had great compassion for the mentally ill, and treated everyone as his equal. Dorothy loved this about him.

I know he will never be canonized, but he was one of the holiest priests I have ever known, and one of the best things he did for me was to introduce me to Dorothy Day. When he died at the age of 77, in 1977, I called Dorothy the next day to tell her, but she had already learned of his passing, and had a Mass offered for him that very morning. She reminded me that years before, Fr. McCoy had offered the first Mass celebrated at their upstate farm in Tivoli, New York. I was with him on that day, and had the good fortune to interview her. It was on May 13, 1964, and here is an excerpt from the transcript of that tape recorded interview.

JC: Today, I have the pleasure and honor to be sitting with Dorothy Day in upstate New York. Dorothy, you moved from your Staten Island farm to the farm here in Tivoli, and I'd like to begin at the beginning. How did the Catholic Worker movement begin?

DD: Well, I've written in the first chapters of the book, *Loaves and Fishes*, a good deal about Peter Maurin. I had worked with the Socialists and Communists for 10 years, and then when I became a Catholic I did some research work for the American Association of University Women; I worked for the movies writing dialogue and synopsizing books and things of that sort, but was searching for work to do within the framework of the Church, along the same lines as I had before...

I prayed so much about these things, about a way opening up, and going on this trip to Washington, D.C., to cover the hunger march and the farmer's convention and prayed down there at the National Shrine that some way would open up to me, by which I could work to improve the social order. And when I came back I found Peter Maurin, thank heaven, waiting for me.

He had been a Christian Brother. He came over here to this country at the time of the expulsion of his Order from France. From the first account, he explained how he traveled over the border illegally with the lumber camps, and worked at every kind of heavy labor, railroad work, road work, worked in the cities as a janitor, servant, and studied constantly and also taught French.

JC: Essentially, what is the idea behind the Catholic Worker movement?

DD: Peter had read some articles I'd written for *Time* magazine and then Joy Schuster advised him to come see me. The Irish Communist Newspaper in Union Square had also advised him to come and visit me because he said our ideas had much in common. So that's why he arrived on the scene.

Peter would start right in talking about some vital problem plunging right into the middle of it. So he plunged into the middle of his program and it was very simple. It was one of reaching people through the works of mercy. The works of mercy would include writing tracts for clarification, running houses of hospitality in parishes, and starting farming communes. That was the very simple outline of his program.

JC: By reaching people, you mean people in need?

DD: No, it was not a question of reaching the people in need. No, Peter was thinking in other terms. He was thinking in terms of making the people think and work out their own problems and work them from the standpoint of the people themselves, not going out to dole out to the people what they needed, but finding what stimulates them into recognizing what their freedom meant. He encouraged people to use their freedom to change their surroundings. He felt, with Jefferson, that he governs best who governs least. He spoke only in terms of man's freedom. That's what stimulated him.

JC: Would you describe him as reacting against anything in particular? This was somewhere around the time of the Great Depression, in the 1930's. Was that an issue with him?

DD: Perhaps he was reacting against the Church's program of always accepting the status quo, and recommending the works of mercy to alleviate the needs of people, but doing nothing to change the social order, which creates these needs.

I think he felt that ideas were meant to bring about revolutions. He was very much interested in getting people stimulated by these ideas. He felt that man had these tremendous capacities in himself that could be developed. He really had a faith in man, you see. He was capable of doing this and he felt very strongly that man had lost his philosophy of work; and that he was only thinking in terms of wages and hours. He felt that men should be thinking more in terms of the common good, and that they should think of work, not as something monotonous and to be put up with for the sake of attaining a salary, but something which made them share in God's plan.

JC: In some ways you and Peter had come along different routes to a common vision. Obviously you met a kindred spirit in Peter, and he in you. What were you searching for at that time?

DD: I wasn't searching for a kindred spirit. No, I don't think Peter and I were kindred spirits. What interested me was his whole attitude with the poor and the man in the street and the worker. My idea was only in terms of unions, the organization of workers, and the class war. I was still very much filled with that whole concept of the social order and Peter Maurin wasn't at all. Peter was really so much the peasant. He thought more of that aspect of his program than anything else. The works of mercy and the houses of hospitality were all raised toward the idea of decentralization; in order to bring about a complete change in the social order.

JC: You're very much aware, I'm sure, that over the years you've not only had critics, but also a few enemies. I've heard people say that your ideals are unrealistic. Others say you are gradually moving away from the world in order to find peace and security.

DD: Well, I think that accusation against the Catholic Worker is certainly ridiculous. It never has retreated from the cities; it's never retreated from the farms. It's in closer contact with reality than all our critics, most certainly. We live with it from year to year. There's no possibility of sentimentality or of a lack of it; it's very hardheaded reality, all our work.

We recognize the difficulties, the problems much more clearly than anybody else, it seems to me. Because this whole program is to be brought about not by the use of force but by the exercise of man's free will, free choice.

JC: The people associated with the Worker for years now have been at the forefront of demonstrations involving nonviolent resistances to various injustices. I wonder if you have felt that in some way you might have been influential in moving society more toward that kind of activity, protest movements in general.

DD: These are the means that always have been used in the labor movement. No, we've only used the tactics of picketing that have also been used in the labor movement because that's the only way open for a great many people to be heard. Pamphleteering has also been a tried and true technique.

JC: You mentioned the Church in this connection. I know that people in positions of Church authority have often misunderstood you. I think it's true to say that you've also been misunderstood by Catholic lay people. Have you found the Church, as it exists, to be a problem or has it helped you?

DD: I found such infinite freedom in the Church, really. And all these controversies, it seems to me, and as Peter always used to point out, were only for clarification of thought. It just seems to me, to be your conscience at work. You try to work out these things. This is the work of the laity, not the clergy.

Father O'Dwyer said that the problem with the American Church was the domineering clergy and the subservient laity. I wasn't acquainted with that, you see. Coming in as a convert all I could see was the beauty of the Church, the writings within the Church. St. Augustine was one of my favorites, of course, and I took it for granted that you worked in your field and that I worked in mine, in the field of the laity. And I took it for granted there'd be a great difference of opinion. That didn't bother me any. I never felt as though I were going against the Church by accepting myself, and my conscience.

I do think the laity has a tremendous role to play, and that we all have these things to work out. Any difference of opinion bothers some of them very much.

I met three Jews at St. Louis University who said to me that two of them had become Catholics... not because they agreed with the Catholic Worker, but because it showed them what a tremendous freedom there was in the Church. They'd been afraid before then. They didn't make a gesture toward it for fear they'd be told how to vote, or what point of view to hold, and so on.

JC: That seems to be the great truth that the Worker has always taught, just by existing, that there is room for so much diversity of thought in the Church. But I'm conscious of the fact that being on the extreme wing of thought in the Church, you will have to endure much criticism and misunderstanding.

DD: I don't exactly know what you're getting at, but I do think there is tremendous freedom in the Church. Christ never coerced anybody. He put up with everything. He put up with the stupid apostles who were still arguing about when He was going to bring in the kingdom, and where they could sit, on the right hand or the left, the whole idea of power. He seemed to have made no impression on them whatever, of the Holy Spirit... but there was no question of any coercion.

Some of the laity tried to help our House of Hospitality, but they were told by the Chancery office not to. Well, of course, my answer to that would be no one could tell a layperson not to perform the works of mercy. You just go ahead and do the work that you feel called upon to do. In Chicago, also, the conscientious objectors who were working in the Alexian Brothers Hospital were told by the Chancery office not to stay at our House of Hospitality. It didn't bother them too much. I didn't think it was that important to make an issue over it.

JC: You mentioned before a theme which is very much in the forefront today, the issue of lay involvement... as recently as two weeks ago in May of '64, Pope Paul VI spoke about our lay apostolate, and encouraged the hierarchy to acknowledge that the layman must be given responsibility in the mission of the Church even independently of the actual direct supervision of the hierarchy or the Chancery office, as you put it.

Do you have any hope that the Second Vatican Council is going to promote a greater activity on the part of lay people?

DD: I think that one of the big problems is to instill in people a sense of their own freedom again. Bishop O'Hara at Kansas City told Peter Maurin to lead the way, and we'll follow. Now that's a very startling statement for a bishop to make. What he meant was there has to be some sort of a vanguard to explore the field and to go ahead and to look into all the possibilities of action. To try to clarify things and to be free to make mistakes.

There are many fields, many fields in which we can work together. But in Pope John's statement he talked about putting it all under the direction of the hierarchy. But how are we to work under the direction of the hierarchy when the hierarchy doesn't know about which side has the most vested interest, if you want to put it that way. Any strike that comes up, as soon as they begin to yell communism at the strikers, well then the Church listens to the people who are accusing strikers of being communists. Whether it's the Singer sewing machine strike or the hospital strikers or the national maritime strikers, I mean, do the Church-men listen to the people who are on strike, or do they listen to the people who are the moneyed parishioners. If you follow the direction of the hierarchy there you couldn't do very much regarding the justice issue.

JC: Dorothy, a lot of people who might read this and hear your references to communism and to communist writers, might wonder why you have that particular orientation. It might give rise to questions about the extent that communism has been an influence in your own life. I know your history, but I just wonder if you might comment on it for our readers?

DD: I don't think anybody in this world is as afraid of communism as Americans are. We're the furthest away from them, but here they are all lined up saying the communists are bad and we're good. And I think that's utter nonsense. To get back a little to the simplicity of the Gospel, that we're supposed to love our enemies, love those who are in error, and think in terms of finding some areas of concordance and agreement with them. I think also in terms of converting them, that's what always strikes me, after all, as a convert. The idea of an absolute lack of hope along those lines is wrong. We just assume that these people will never change. St. Paul wouldn't have preached the Gospel if he didn't believe in the conversion of hearts.

I think we have to learn what to do, how to work together, learn something about coexistence.

We had some very good articles on coexistence in the *Catholic Worker* many years ago. I think people should be reading the Pope's encyclical, *Pacem in Terris*. I think he's brought many ideas of how we can go ahead and work in a social order.

I thought it was certainly the way a Pope should be. Having a sense of being the pastor, a shepherd of the whole world. I think most priests don't realize that they are supposed to be speaking in terms of their whole parish. Everybody in the parish, whether they're communists or not, whether they lack loved ones or not, they are all souls, all human beings, and they all should be of concern to us.

JC: I'm going to change the topic for a minute. You have lived in a very busy atmosphere; I'm wondering how the din and distraction of all the activity at the soup kitchen affects you and your prayer life.

DD: I feel very free, of course, to take off, and get away from it all. We do have privacy. We need it terribly because we are living in very close quarters most of the time. This is the most space we've ever had in our lives here at Tivoli, and everybody knows that as soon as a retreat begins, or a lecture series, we become crowded. We all have to get together and share one room.

And you have to take what you need. With a good examination of conscience you find that there is time for yourself. It isn't other people that are keeping you from studying, from prayer. It's very often your own difficult temperament. And when you get to that phase, you look to yourself first of all, and take the time. You begin to get things straightened out in your mind.

I say to myself, well why should I be worrying about the kitchen, the way it's managed? Why should I be worrying about the shopping? Why should I be worrying about anything else? If I tend to my own knitting and do my own job, and go in and answer the letters that I've got piled up on my desk, and do the reading I used to do, after all there's a tremendous amount of study, a tremendous amount of work to be done, and articles to be written here and there. Well, if you do the work that you have to do yourself, you won't have any problems with the place itself.

But you have to do that over and over again. I think in any community, you have to be constantly getting back, and taking care of your own affairs, minding your own business, and doing your own particular job. And if you do that well, then you begin to have a different perspective on everybody else. You haven't got time for so much criticism.

That's terribly important, looking after yourself first of all, and not worrying about other people's spiritual development. For one thing we scarcely know ourselves, let alone anybody else around us.

JC: Dorothy, you're familiar with the regime of discipline in religious life. Bells ring and it's time to pray, or eat, or go to recreation. Does your apostolate operate like that?

DD: We have enough of that in our community life. When a bell rings you go to dinner whether you want to eat or not, because dinner is served at that hour. When Mass is offered at a certain time you go to Mass. You have to keep a routine. Any family is governed, maybe not by bells, but they're governed by the children around them. There's a great deal of safety in that. Everybody tends to isolate himself or herself. They have their own little apartment, and want to do as they please. They're not thinking in terms of the community. It takes an immense amount of time to join in, but I think in a community you're governed more or less by the needs of the community. Just like a family. The husband can't think of himself alone. Your choices narrow in life. They are more or less laid out for you by your choice of vocation.

JC: So you favor the bells and the discipline.

DD: Yes. I think the routine laid down by a convent isn't anything to criticize. When the bell rings you go to pray. Well, you may not be able to pray, but you can at least relax, and express the prayers that you're supposed to say at that time. I mean, after all, you often have to talk when you don't feel like talking. You have to make conversation at meals, responding to people. This is like being obedient to every living creature, as St. Paul said.

I need to begin my day with very definite prayers, like the Angelus, and the Veni Creator, the Creed, the Our Father, the Hail Mary and so on. These prayers gave me great comfort when I became a Catholic. I felt that there was a rule of life, and I feel it is a tremendous aid to teach you those set forms, like you wash your face in the morning, and brush your teeth, and you come to life again.

Cardinal Newman had a simple rule of life; it included Mass and Communion, the Rosary, and doing some spiritual reading. It's a routine you don't neglect. I think the lay breviary (the daily prayers of the Church) is wonderful.

JC: What about spontaneous prayer, and the relationship between prayer and the beauty of nature?

DD: The soul needs exercise as well as the body. Prayer is as necessary for the soul as breathing is for the body. You shouldn't neglect the routine forms of prayer. A lot of it is spontaneous of course, but you shouldn't neglect prayer routines. Just to walk along the seashore is a prayer. I think most people respond to beauty by giving thanksgiving or praise of God. True prayer comes from the appreciation of beauty. That's why it's so wonderful to have a place like this.

You can find beauty even in the cities and in the crowds. Not if you walk along with your head in the air, but if you look, you'll find beauty in the children playing on the street, in the feather of a pigeon on the ground. Beauty is everywhere and it has a tremendous influence on people. Some people walk along the beach but they never see a shell. They have no sense of it. A sense of beauty is so necessary. To love something you first have to know it.

I am making a study of herbs and weeds. Peggy and I are always stealing a particular book from one another on herbs. It goes back and forth because it's a very interesting study. I think things like that contribute to your spiritual life. It all points to the Creator. St. Thomas said, "Certainly the more you know about the created world around you, the more you know God." So that any kind of piety which is full and rounded out by the knowledge of music, literature and poetry, and all the sciences, contributes to the faith, and to the richness of the spiritual life.

Baron von Hugel said that too, that we are living on two or three levels at the same time, the spiritual level, the physical level, and the intellectual level, and they all balance one another. They need each other.

JC: A lot of people today are struggling in their relationship with God. We meet them time and again, people who are disappointed because they feel a sense of failure and frustration about their inability to see or feel God directly. Did you ever have that feeling? And may I ask, why did you call your autobiography, *The Long Loneliness*?

DD: St. Augustine said, "Our hearts are restless until they rest in Thee, O Lord." He meant that no matter how much we have in life we're never going to see the fullness and completion of the life we yearn for, not in this world. There will always be this desire for more. We are never going to be satisfied.

JC: There seems to be a need for a deeper understanding of that idea. Can you expand on it?

DD: It's not a matter of feelings or emotions. No. The spiritual life may have good feelings and a sense of joy with it, but that's the milk that's fed to the babe. As one grows in the spiritual life, it's very often a desert to traverse, and you need someone to show you the path. I read an article recently that dealt with tedium, and this is a constant problem for people in their spiritual journey. They need to be renewed and refreshed. They need to be fed. If they are not fed they suffer terribly.

Priests have a tremendous responsibility in this. I think the way some priests say Mass is enough to give anybody a nervous breakdown. The tremendous pace and speed of it is a scandal. The name of God means something. The word of God, according to the Old Testament and the New, brings about the presence of God. Just as the Pillar of Fire and the various names of God all have great meaning and deserve great reverence.

The priests are not feeding the faithful. Think of what St. Francis of Assisi said about the sheep that are not fed by the shepherd. It's a terrible thing; one of the great scandals... and certainly the cause of much frustration among the laity in their spiritual life.

JC: How then would you describe a good shepherd?

DD: It sounds funny to say but I think it's more important for the shepherd to be feeding his sheep than it is for him to be out there on a picket line defending a just cause.

The first job of the priest it seems to me is not only to give us the sacraments, but also to give us some knowledge of what it really means, what the sacraments really mean, and how the sacraments feed the soul. Most of us don't develop at all spiritually. We grow physically but not spiritually. And when people console themselves by saying we're not in a state of mortal sin, at least we're in the state of grace, it's like saying to a mother whose child is mentally deficient, at least he has life.

If you don't develop spiritually, if you don't realize that you have arrested this life of God in you, you only have half-a-loaf. You are cheated. Never forget the fact that we're capable of tremendous growth. People aren't told that, they're not taught that. It seems to me for a priest not to tell the laity what the sacraments entail is a shame. At every one of our retreats we renew our Baptismal vows. One fellow said, "I read the vows over each time before I decide to renew them. I mean they entail a great deal."

For instance we've taken this vow to renounce the world, the flesh and the devil, and then we go out and make as much money as possible. Anything is permitted provided you don't fall into mortal sin. It's as though you can go as far as you like, provided you don't go any further. There's no sense to this approach, it leaves no room for spiritual growth in the spiritual life. If it weren't for the life of grace you couldn't enjoy all the other wonderful gifts that God sends.

I think very often to myself, as I travel around the country giving talks, and feeling utterly dull. You say to yourself, well it's my job. It happens to be my duty. I have my particular vocation, and so I do it. But I should be conscious of the fact that it is not me speaking, it is Christ speaking in me. We put on Christ, and we put off the old man, and this change is taking place all the time. We are always growing in His grace.

People say the ideals of the Catholic Worker movement are so unattainable, and all that. It's not as though we have attained anything, but that doesn't mean we should lower our ideals. Living in community is a good and healthy thing, and we always fall short of our ideals, but that doesn't give us the excuse to lower them. You're going to keep going right ahead no matter how far you fall short of them.

I know it used to bother me an awful lot. I'd say how can we say we're Christians, and that we love one another, when there are always conflicts. On one day we see everybody's faults, on another day we see all their virtues. One day we are blind, and see through a glass darkly as St. Paul said, but on another day we'll see very clearly. The point of it is that you don't lower your ideals because of conflicts coming from within or from the outside. But believe me you are tried as though by fire when you're living this way, together over the years. This is now 32 or 33 years.

The same is true with the Church. The Church doesn't lower its ideals. That's one of those things I admire so about it. We may fall far short of our goals, but we go on. The truth is that we don't need to fall so far short. We can do better. We should constantly recognize the fact that we can do far more.

JC: Dorothy, thank you for your time and wisdom. May the Lord abundantly bless you and everyone in your community. Thank you so very much.

I saw Dorothy on and off over the next few years. In 1975 she gave a seminar at the Charismatic Renewal Conference held in Atlantic City, NJ. She was well into her seventies at the time, and suffered from severe arthritis, but on that day, she gave one of her best talks. She spoke of the importance of having love, genuine love, for the poor and homeless. She said that most people disregard the plight of the poor.

Later I managed to talk briefly with her, and I asked what her impressions were of the Charismatic Renewal. She replied, "I am edified coming to this conference, to see so many people with their hearts, arms and voices lifted up in praise and thanksgiving to Almighty God."

Dorothy died of congestive heart failure on November 29, 1980, at Maryhouse, the Catholic Worker house on New York City's Lower East Side. She was 83 years old. I attended her wake along with hundreds of other mourners.

She was a woman of faith, a writer and fighter for justice, a pacifist, and a devoted mother and grandmother. Above all Dorothy was a woman of prayer.

As she lay there in an open pine box, as poor in death as she was in life, I was filled with awe at the sight of her. There was no attempt to disguise the reality of death. No make-up, no fancy fabric in her casket. Her face had a stark and luminous beauty about it.

I recalled when I was a college student how I used to read *The Catholic Worker* newspaper, and how her ideas influenced my future decision to be a priest. I thought I knew what a Christian was until I read her writings, especially her concept of voluntary poverty. She had renounced all her possessions to live among the poor in order to feed them, clothe them and minister to them. She lived the Sermon on the Mount so radically, that her life made thousands of admirers re-examine their own value system.

For Dorothy Day, religion was not a system of beliefs. It was a commitment to Jesus and His social teachings. She lived her ideals without being smug or superior. It was her vocation to practice the works of mercy, oppose violence, run a soup kitchen, and witness to the love of Jesus.

Once she was asked, "What words would you like on your tombstone?" She answered without hesitation: "*Deo Gratias.*"

What you do for the least of my brethren
that you do for me.

Matthew 25:40

4

MOTHER TERESA OF CALCUTTA

In your service to others, keep to the humble works because they are the works nobody else will do. Even if you just go to a lonely person and sit and listen or clean the house like some of our coworkers are doing, it is beautiful. It is never too small for God. Fidelity to the little things helps us to grow in love. A living love hurts. Jesus, to prove His love for us died on the cross. The mother, to give birth to her child, has to suffer; if you really love one another properly, there must be sacrifice.

Agnes Bojaxhiu was born in 1910, of Albanian parents. She joined the Sisters of Loretto in Ireland when she was seventeen, and within a year was sent to teach in Calcutta, India where she experienced the appalling destitution of the people living in the city slums. They literally lived and died in the streets.

In 1948 she left the Sisters of Loretto to serve those sick and dying people. She established the Missionaries of Charity and soon became known as Mother Teresa of Calcutta.

Her words have a special authenticity about them. *"Each person's mission is a mission of love, and the work of love should begin in our own homes. You must have time for your own first, and only after that should your work be for others."* She said that we should *"make our homes centers of compassion and forgive endlessly. Let no one ever come to you without coming away better and happier. Let us begin then in the place where we are, with people with whom we are the closest and then spread out."*

Her philosophy of life was simple: *"At the hour of death, when we come face to face with God, we are going to be judged on love; not on how much we've done, but on how much love we have put into our actions."*

Time magazine once devoted an entire issue to living saints, and Mother Teresa, a Roman Catholic nun, was featured on the cover. She attracted thousands of young women who wanted to work with her among the poor.

Mother Teresa traveled widely, and in her later years became a living legend. Once a reporter called out to her, *"Mother, some people think you are a living saint. How do you feel about that?"* Without missing a beat she replied, *"You sir are called to be holy in what you do, and I am called to be holy in the position that God has put me. So it is nothing extraordinary to be holy in what we do. We all have the same vocation to holiness."*

Her goal was to help the poor and abandoned people of India die with dignity. She directed her sisters to do their work quietly, never preaching or attempting to convert anyone. She said, *"The worst disease of all is the disease of being an unwanted castoff. Our sisters go out with the love that Christ gives to us, and we pass that love on to others. If we were not part of that stream of love, which God is always pouring out, we could not come back here day after day."*

The Hindus believe in the law of Karma. The reason people are left dying in the streets of India has to do with their belief in the notion of reincarnation. They believe that an individual's state in this life is determined by his or her behavior in a former life. If you were good in an earlier life, you will return to a higher form of life in the next one. If you were evil, you will descend to a lower form, perhaps becoming an insect or an animal. If one comes back as a poor beggar, it is merely one's fate or Karma, and no one can save you from it.

Your life, therefore, is either a just punishment for past failures, or a just reward for former acts of virtue. The Hindu equivalent of heaven is called Nirvana. Once you break through the cycle of reincarnation, you are absorbed into the great Brahma. This return to God is like a drop of water returning to the ocean. Your individuality is snuffed out. This is their idea of heaven.

Until you attain this concept of heaven, you are expected to endure the misery of your present state, no matter what it is. Therefore, those suffering in the streets of Calcutta, or anywhere else, are of no concern to the Hindu, who views them dispassionately since their life now is the inevitable consequence of their past lives. They are merely living out their destiny.

This is why the Hindu appears to be untroubled by the sight of hunger, disease or death. Nevertheless, the Hindus admired Mother Teresa immensely for caring for the sick. Mother believed in the words of Jesus, *"What you do for the least of your brothers, you do for Me"* (Matthew 25:40). She often said that Jesus comes to us in distressing disguises. An emaciated woman, gasping for breath in the gutter, cannot be ignored. Even though Hindus think that she is living out her Karma, Mother Teresa saw her as Christ suffering on the cross. In serving the poor, she and her sisters were serving Christ, in a mystical way.

I met Mother Teresa for the first time in 1980. It was the same time I was in Rome with Cardinal Leon-Josef Suenens. Mother was also attending. The gathering was dedicated to Family Life, and she was an expert in that field.

One of the high points of that busy week was spotting Mother Teresa amid all the men in red and purple vestments. She was wearing that familiar white sari trimmed with blue. She was with one other sister from her community.

I went over to her at the break, and introduced myself. She was gracious, and was willing to chat.

JC: What are your hopes for the Synod?

MT: I hope family life could be improved. Families should be places of love. Husbands and wives should love one another, and parents should really love their children as Christ would love them. It is not enough for us to say, "I love God." St. John says you are a liar if you say you love God and you do not love your neighbor. It is very important for us to realize that love, to be true, has to hurt. I must be willing to give whatever it takes not to harm others, in fact to do good to them. This requires that we give until it hurts. Otherwise it is not true love.

Jesus made Himself hungry, poor, naked and homeless to save us from our selfishness and sin.

JC: Could you comment on family life?

MT: I appeal everywhere for parents to look after the child. The child is God's gift to the family. Every child is created in God's image. We must bring the child back to the center of our care. This is the only way our world can survive because our children are the only hope we have for the future.

The greatest destroyer of peace today is abortion because it is a war against the child, a direct killing of the innocent child, murdered by the mother herself. If we accept that a mother can kill her own child, how can we tell other people not to kill one another? We must persuade her with love and remind ourselves that love means to be willing to give even until it hurts. We are fighting abortion by adoption, by caring for the mothers and helping in the adoption of her baby. We have saved thousands of lives. We beg the mothers, "Please don't kill the child. Give me the child and I will find a good home for the child to be loved in."

Jesus gave His life to love us. So the mother who is thinking about abortion should be helped to love until it hurts. She needs to respect the life of the child within. Any country that accepts abortion is not teaching its people to love, but rather to use violence to get what they want.

The father of that child must also be ready to give until it hurts.

JC: Do you have any comments about the treatment of the elderly in families?

MT: I can never forget the experience I had in visiting an assisted living home where they kept all these old parents in an institution. Some of their own children forgot about them. The old people had everything – good food, comfortable furniture, television, but everyone was looking toward the door. I did not see a single smile. "Why are they not smiling?" I asked a sister near me.

I'm so used to seeing smiles, even the dying ones smile. And sister said, "This is the way it is nearly every day. They are hurt because they are forgotten."

You see, this kind of neglect to love, brings with it spiritual poverty. Many in our own families are sick, or are feeling worried. Are we there to help? Are we willing to give until it hurts? Or do we put our own interests first? These are questions all family members must ask themselves.

If we are true Christians, these problems should never discourage us. I talk so often about giving with a smile.

Keep the joy of loving Jesus in your heart, and share that joy with others.

JC: Thank you, Mother.

I think Mother Teresa of Calcutta was one of the greatest saints of the twentieth century. Even the secular media extolled her holiness.

I was pleasantly surprised in 1990 when her community invited me to give a nine-day retreat to her contemplative novices. In case you might not know it, Mother Teresa's community is divided into two divisions: one group is dedicated to active service among the poor; the contemplative branch is dedicated totally to prayer. The retreat I gave was for the novices of the contemplative branch.

Mother Teresa had the local superior send me their constitution to guide me in preparing for that retreat, which was held in the convent of St. Mary's parish in Plainfield, New Jersey.

Here are a few excerpts from the constitution:

> *"The mission is to proclaim Jesus to all nations. Our community is committed to wholehearted and free service to the poorest of the poor, and to the perfect love of God and neighbor.*
> *"So that the Church may shine forth as a people made one with the unity of the Father, Son, and Holy Spirit, we live in community.*
> *"Our particular mission is to labor for the salvation and sanctification of the poorest of the poor, not only in the slums, but also all over the world wherever they may be... that the Church may be fully present in the world."*

As I stood before this group of young women, with a few exceptions of late vocations, I recalled Mother Teresa's answer to the question "Do you have a say in the acceptance of all your sisters, and if so what criteria do you use in making your decision?" She quickly replied, "Yes, I see everyone of them, and I try to find out if they are happy. If they are happy, I accept them; if not, I send them home."

Perhaps this is why I found her community to be filled with joy. Their deep piety made a profound impression on me.

Contemplatives are usually confined within the convent walls, but her sisters are allowed to go outdoors for about two hours a day. They go two by two, not for recreation or to do social work, but to visit homes in the neighborhood. They knock on doors asking people if they have anyone they would like the sisters to pray for. Very often they pray with the families on the spot, or they visit their sick members. They often comfort those who are in sorrow.

The community is called, "Missionaries of Divine Love." Each day they rise at 4:30 a.m. for prayerful meditation and Mass. Those who belong to the active branch, like the ones ministering on the streets of Calcutta, India, go to work after breakfast, and spend the whole day among the poor. One day a week each sister, alternately, spends the entire day at home, resting and in prayer.

Mother Teresa characterized their apostolate as one of "presence." She believes that love is being present to those in need: "The best way to prove our love and gratitude to Mother Church is by striving sincerely and earnestly to be true witnesses of her holiness in the world."

She always believed that the Church, with all its faults, is a refuge of sinners and a port in the storm of life. To her, the Church is Jesus Christ ministering to those in need in today's world.

Mother Teresa's vision made such an impact on Indian society that the Indian government gave her their highest national honor, a military funeral. It was somewhat incongruous that a woman of peace should lie in state surrounded by armed soldiers, but so it was. She received India's highest sign of respect. There will never again be anyone like her.

People are not looking for a Church
that panders to them, but one that challenges
them to be completely open to Christ.

Pope Benedict XVI

5

ARCHBISHOP FULTON J. SHEEN

The possession of one virtue in an eminent degree no more makes a man great than one wing makes a bird fly... A really great character is not just a brave man, for if a man were brave without being tender, he might very easily become cruel... Love for peace alone does not make character, for without the opposite virtue of courage, peacefulness could very easily slip into spineless cowardice.

Fulton Sheen was a kind man, but he was not afraid to challenge people.

Born in 1895, Bishop Sheen was best known as a TV personality during the 1950's. His program, "Life Is Worth Living," was immensely successful, reaching a TV audience of over thirty million viewers.

Ordained for the Peoria, Illinois Diocese in 1919, he did graduate studies at the Catholic University of America, Washington, D.C., and received a Ph.D. in Philosophy from the University of Louvain, Belgium, in 1923.

He was appointed to the faculty of Catholic University in 1926, and taught philosophy there until 1950. He was a featured speaker on "The Catholic Hour," a national radio broadcast, with an estimated audience of four million listeners. This led to his weekly television show, which lasted from 1951-1957.

In 1950 he became the national director of the Society for the Propagation of the Faith, and raised millions of dollars for the missions. On October 26, 1966, Pope Paul VI made Fulton J. Sheen the Bishop of Rochester, New York. He was seventy-one at the time he reached this pinnacle; it was the culmination of almost fifty years of dedicated service to the Catholic Church.

His fame as a television preacher stayed with him throughout his entire life, and made him one of this nation's – and the world's – best known and loved Catholic priests. Statesmen, educators, and clergymen throughout the world held him in high esteem. He authored sixty books; his appeal seemed to be universal.

Our nation is made up of members of many different religions and ideologies, and Fulton Sheen, a priest from Peoria, Illinois, seemed to cut across many layers of society. He touched the lives of ordinary people of all faiths, and of no particular faith.

I met him a few times when he was a monsignor in New York City, serving as the Director of the Propagation of the Faith. The first time was in 1955 when I was discharged from the Army. I had finally decided to enter the seminary, but I didn't know whether to become a diocesan priest, that is a parish priest, or to join a religious community like the Jesuits or the Paulists.

Making that decision tormented me for months after I got out of the Army. As it turned out a relative of mine worked at the Hotel Roosevelt in New York City where Fulton Sheen often came. My uncle bragged about knowing the famous television priest, so l asked him if he could arrange an appointment for me to meet Sheen. He agreed, and it was arranged within a week.

When I arrived, I was invited to wait in his office. The walls of the room were lined with rows of his own books. I sat nervously for about ten minutes, and finally Sheen entered the room in the full episcopal attire that I had seen on TV many times.

I was a little nervous, but he put me at ease, and I tried to explain my problem which seemed more and more insignificant as I spoke about it. And yet, I hoped that through this man, God would tell me where I was going to spend the rest of my life. So it was an important moment for me.

He patiently listened, but made no suggestions about which community to enter or which diocese to go to. Instead he advised me to pray to God for three signs in the next week or so. He said it might be a letter from someone I hadn't heard from for years, or an invitation to some event that would put me in contact with a person who might guide me more directly. His basic answer was this: pray about it.

Since I had been doing that for some time, I felt more confused than ever. However, I agreed that I would pray more about it. I remember that he acted as though God was directly concerned with my problem, and would be ready to guide me once I asked Him to send me some sign. It was not exactly the answer I expected, but it did make sense.

I thanked him as I left, but had a tinge of doubt about whether or not this would really work. To make a long story short, within two weeks it did. I actually became convinced that God wanted me to become a diocesan priest. The idea of offering Holy Mass in a parish setting suddenly appealed to me in a new way. The thought of being a priest teaching in a college, or doing some special work that is often associated with religious communities, no longer appealed to me.

I never received any letter, or met any new person. However, by attending Mass in my parish and observing the parish priests fulfill their duties, I was attracted to the ordinary life of the parish priest and felt the issue was settled. Perhaps it was Bishop Sheen's prayers that turned the tide. He promised to pray for me, and I believe he helped me in a way I can never quite explain.

In reading Bishop Sheen's books over the years, I remember one dominant idea that he taught, namely, that *"character is the balanced tension between opposite virtues.*" He questioned the idea that any single virtue can make any man great. He insisted that there must be some contrasting virtues. He loved to challenge people in unusual ways:

> *We can no longer live on crossword puzzles, television, deodorants. We simply cannot! We have had a thousand excuses. We have fiery urges; we say that we must satisfy them. Or we are used to our grand style of living; therefore, we cannot let our wealth go. Is not our Christian world in danger of being stuck with our electric can openers, our Cadillacs, our cocktails before dinner – not because they are bad in themselves, but because they are being used to fill up our empty lives, instead of caring for those in need.*

He was kind and courteous to his adoring fans, but he could be curt and short-tempered when he detected an abuse of some kind. After he retired from his post in Rochester, New York in 1969, he became increasingly critical of certain post-Vatican II developments.

Once in 1970, he came to preach at a parish close to me in Clifton, New Jersey, and opened with this remark: "*Ladies, gentlemen and recognizable sisters.*" It was a dig at the nuns who were changing from their traditional habits to dress in civilian clothes. He added fuel to the fire when he told the audience that he had passed by a pawnshop in New York City once, where he saw a tray full of crucifixes for sale. He said he went in to inquire where the crosses came from. The shop attendant said that a group of nuns had sold them to him. Then Sheen's eyes blazed as he shouted, "*FOR THIRTY PIECES OF SILVER!*"

Bishop Sheen had an interesting way of posing his questions:

58

Why is it that something not at all funny on the street can be very funny in Church? If a bishop wears a miter cocked on the side of his head in Church, it is very amusing, but if you see a man on the street with his hat cocked to one side, you don't pay any attention to it. The crooked miter is funny because of the seriousness of Christ and the Church.

Pleasure is best when it comes as a kind of treat or surprise. People who are always bent on having a good time, never have a good time, because they have no contrast with what is a good time. If every day were the Fourth of July, nobody would enjoy firecrackers; and if every day were Christmas, no one would enjoy the feast.

The Bishop was wise in so many ways:

It is interesting that most of our relationships with other people are contacts, as one billiard ball contacts another billiard ball. We become like oranges in a box; we mingle with others externally, but do not commune with others in a common task: "news of the hour, on the hour" keeps us buried in the trivialities of external stimuli, lulling us into the belief that we are in contact with reality. The inner life is never given a moment to see ourselves as we really are.

His spiritual advice was often very simple:

The purpose of life is not pleasure. Rather, it is to attain to perfect life, all truth and undying ecstatic love – and this is the definition of God. In pursuing that goal we find happiness. Pleasure is not the purpose of anything; pleasure is a by-product resulting from doing something that is good. One of the best ways to get happiness and pleasure out of life is to ask ourselves, How can I please God? And, why am

I not better? It is the pleasure-seekers who are bored, for all pleasures diminish with their repetition.

He made this wonderful observation about loneliness:

The basic cause of loneliness is the excessive desire to be loved, for this creates a loveless atmosphere. The more we seek to be loved, the less we are loved. The less we are loved, the less lovable we become. And the less lovable we become, the less capable we become of loving anyone else. Like a bird caught in a net, we deepen our own tragedy.
The most immediate cure for loneliness is to show kindness to others. The search for happiness, by turning one's back on humanity, kills happiness. The slums, the city hospitals, the missions, the unloved, the ugly, the socially disinherited – all these are potential remedies for the darkest of souls.

Once I interviewed Milton Berle, the famous television comedian, and he quipped, "You know, it was Bishop Sheen who knocked me off on my ratings; we were opposite one another at the same time every Tuesday night."

I replied, "I didn't realize that." Berle shot back, "Yes, but he had better writers..." "Better writers?" I asked. "Come on Father," he quipped, "Matthew, Mark, Luke, and John."

Uncle Milton was witty, but I learned later that he had stolen that very line from Bishop Sheen himself. It was during an Emmy Award program, and Gary Moore, a variety show host, received a television award for his spontaneity, at which time he said, "I want to pay tribute to the four guys responsible for my spontaneity – my writers."

The next person in line to receive an Emmy that evening was Bishop Sheen, who first thanked the presenter and then said, "I also want to pay tribute to my writers – Matthew, Mark, Luke, and John!" I wonder if Sheen and Gary Moore cooked up that joke before the show went on the air. It wouldn't surprise me.

Archbishop Fulton Sheen was a celebrity, a TV preacher, and a humble priest of Jesus Christ. He was a true messenger of God's love and truth in our modern world and, at least in part for this reason, he is being seriously considered for canonization.

The Spirit helps us in our weakness.
For we do not know how to pray as we should
but the Spirit Himself intercedes for us
with sighs that cannot be put into words.

Romans 8:26

6

CATHERINE DE HUECK DOHERTY

*I know Lord, I cannot turn back. I have heard the beating
of your heart. I have realized your love for me. I will follow
you unto the end, with your help. The graces you send me
are here because I am so weak. Others can rely on their good
lives – their good works. I rely on you, for I have nothing to
offer you except that love that you kindled in my heart one
dark night when I was at the edge of a precipice.*

Catherine Doherty, also known as the Baroness de Hueck, was
born Catherine Kolyschkine in Russia in 1896. Those closest to
her called her the "B," for "Baroness." A group of children from
Harlem once dubbed her "The Bee who brings us honey." She was
both a shy contemplative, and a woman of action. Sometimes she
could be a strict authoritarian, at other times she became a simple
child. Depending on the circumstances, she acted decisively, or
not at all. She was truly a complex person.

It was in Combermere, a township in one of Ontario's most
economically depressed areas, that I first met Catherine de Hueck
Doherty. By the time I arrived, she had already attracted many
followers who joined her in dedicating their lives to "living the
Gospel without compromise." Their community is known as

Madonna House, and it has become the headquarters for an international movement.

They came from all over the world and stayed through the austere Canadian winters. She called them staff workers, and prepared them to take promises of poverty, chastity and obedience. One of the main tasks was taking care of the countless young adults who flocked to Madonna House year after year. The community became a port in the storm of life for many of the kids who arrived exhausted and in need of spiritual help. They came for psychological help as well, and received an abundance of love.

Madonna House is a spiritual community of celibate men and women, living together in peace and harmony. The men work the farms, build the barns, and repair the machinery, while the women do the cooking, the sewing, the laundry and innumerable tasks that create an atmosphere of emotional comfort.

The centerpiece of each day is the Holy Sacrifice of the Mass, which is offered alternately by one of the many priest members of the community. Madonna House has matured to the point where it is now sending out priests and staff workers to missions all over the world. At this writing they have 23 houses established on five continents. Catherine made the rule that they would only go to countries where they were invited by the local bishops to serve in various capacities at the bishop's direction. Most of the houses they open today are "listening houses," as the B called them, places where people can come to talk and pray in a quasi-contemplative setting.

When I first came to Madonna House I was deeply moved by the spirit of love and holiness I found there, especially among the staff workers. I made up my mind to return the next summer and I kept coming back each summer for 28 years.

The spirituality of Catherine de Hueck Doherty became the inspiration behind this amazing community.

As a child of the Russian aristocracy, Catherine grew up in a home which was steeped in the traditions of the Russian Orthodox Church. She traveled all over Russia, Europe, and Egypt before she was a teenager, learning six languages in the process. At age 15, her family arranged her marriage to Baron Boris de Hueck. As a young woman she served as an army nurse during World War I.

When the Communist Revolution of 1917 hit, she and her aristocratic family had to flee from Russia. They were rounded up, imprisoned, and sentenced to death by starvation. Catherine promised God that she would spend her life serving the poor if she and her husband could escape. The miracle happened, and they did escape.

Catherine and Boris fled first to Canada where she had to work at menial jobs to support her ailing husband and infant son. She was fortunate enough to climb up on the economic ladder, when an agent asked her to join his lecture tour, and talk about the Russian Revolution. She gradually gained economic security, but was still tormented by the promise she made to God that if He would help her escape she would give her life in service to Him.

She was deeply touched by the words of the Gospel: *"Arise – and go! Sell everything you possess... give it to the poor... and come follow Me."*

Yielding to this call, she decided to keep her promise by working directly among the poorest of the poor. In 1930 she established Friendship House in Toronto. The local clergy were not happy about a laywoman beginning a lay apostolate on her own. The Depression years were hard on everyone, and she was virtually forced to leave Canada. It took courage to begin again, but she moved to Harlem in New York City. With the permission of the local Church authorities she became a pioneer in the cause of inter-racial justice. Later she opened a new Friendship House in Chicago.

It was there that she met the Irish-American journalist, Eddie Doherty, who won her heart. She had been separated from her Russian husband for some time since he left her. She was able to obtain an ecclesiastical annulment from that marriage. It had been an arranged union as was the custom among the Russian aristocracy. She was only fifteen at the time, and said she did not give her consent willingly. Once she was free, she and Eddie Doherty married in Bishop Sheil's chapel in Chicago in 1943. They moved to Combermere, Canada in 1947. After she had visited with the Bishop of Pembroke, Canada, he encouraged her to start a rural apostolate in his diocese. She and Eddie began to serve the needs of the local people in this new setting.

The Catholic faith was strong in Canada, and soon many young men and women began coming to this new ministry, which Catherine called Madonna House. Before long, to Catherine's surprise, a few priests came looking to the growing community.

Without any preconceived plans, and driven only by her love for the poor, Catherine accepted everyone with open arms.

In 1952, she managed to get a private audience with Pope Pius XII, who asked her about her young community. He suggested that Madonna House should apply for the status of a secular institute, i.e., a community where the members take vows to live a life of poverty, chastity, and obedience.

Catherine's life story has been told in greater detail in two books that Eddie Doherty wrote: *Tumbleweed* and *Cricket in My Heart*. She also wrote her own autobiography entitled, *Fragments of My Life*, where she tells bits and pieces of her life story. The most comprehensive biography of her is Lorene Hanley Duquin's *They Called Her the Baroness* (St Pauls/Alba House, 1995). At her request I wrote the Introduction to the book.

To understand Catherine more fully, it is important to learn about her husband Eddie Doherty, a very holy man. Born in 1890, he had a successful career as a journalist, working for many newspapers and magazines. Among other things, he wrote the screen-play for *The Fighting Sullivans*. In the latter part of their marriage they decided voluntarily to live apart in a brother/sister relationship. They had taken the same vows that all the members of the Madonna House staff took, namely, poverty, chastity and obedience. The founding couple wanted to be on the same level of the young, single men and women in the community.

This arrangement was in place for thirteen years, when Eddie, in his late seventies, was invited to study for the priesthood.

This came about through his friendship with Archbishop Joseph Raya of the Melkite rite. As a young priest, Father Raya visited Combermere, fell in love with the spirit of Madonna House, and decided to join the community as an associate priest. One time he promised Eddie that if he ever became a bishop, he would ordain him.

When Father Raya was consecrated an archbishop in a beautiful ceremony in Birmingham conducted by Patriarch Maximos V. Hakim, Eddie remembered that promise and asked, "Well, Archbishop, now that you're a big shot, what are you going to do about that promise?" "I meant it, Eddie, give me a little time."

And so it was, after a few years of training, Eddie Doherty was ordained a deacon in Nazareth, the very town where Christ had grown to manhood. It was on the 26th anniversary of his marriage to Catherine. He was ordained to the priesthood in the Melkite rite two months later on August 15, 1969, the Feast of the Assumption of the Blessed Virgin Mary. He was 79 years old.

The Melkite rite has an ancient tradition of ordaining married men so there was no problem on that score. After his ordination Eddie lived for a while in the Episcopal Residence in Haifa, located at the foot of Mount Carmel, with the hills of Lebanon visible on the distant horizon. He decided to return home to Canada, and live out his remaining years as a priest of the Madonna House community.

I visited Catherine in the summer of 1985 as she was dying a slow, lingering death. We chatted for a while, and she whispered to me, *"Father John you are a good priest, but you could be better."*

I thought to myself, "Amen sister." I still smile at the memory of that visit. She had a way of challenging everyone right down to her last breath.

Catherine died on December 14, 1985 at the age of 89. Her husband Eddie had died ten years earlier at Victoria Hospital in Renfrew, Canada on May 3, 1975. He was 84.

Catherine believed that no part of the Gospel is abstract. The ordinariness of daily life is the warp and woof of living the Gospel without compromise. This was her way of restoring the world to Christ.

A carpenter works with wood. A computer operator works with computers. A cook feeds the community. The idea is that one's spirituality can be incarnated into every daily routine. Just as Jesus Christ the Son of God lived a simple life, so we live the Gospel with our hands, our minds, and our hearts, as we go about our daily tasks. Whether it is sewing on a button, typing a letter, or milking a cow, the vocation of those at Madonna House is to do little things well for the love of God. Anyone who wants to follow Christ's example will agree with this formula. The simple life of Jesus during His time at Nazareth was what Catherine envisioned as the goal of Madonna House.

She believed that fidelity to the ordinary, daily things of life, the "duty of the moment," leads to sanctity, and the restoration of the world to the Lord.

A synopsis of her spiritual message is found in her "Little Mandate," which consists of eight points. Using the words of Jesus, she formulated this directive:

Arise – go! Sell all you possess... give it directly, personally to the poor. Take up My cross (their cross) and follow Me – going to the poor – being poor – being one with them – one with Me.

1. *Always be little... simple – poor – childlike.*
2. *Preach the Gospel WITH YOUR LIFE – WITHOUT COMPROMISE – listen to the Spirit – He will lead you.*
3. *Do little things exceedingly well for the love of Me.*
4. *Love – love – love, never counting the cost.*
5. *Go into the marketplace and stay with Me... pray... fast... pray always... fast.*
6. *Be hidden – be a light to your neighbor's feet. Go without fears into the depth of men's hearts... I shall be with you.*

One of the great gifts of Catherine to the Western Church was the experience of the *Poustinia*, which is the Russian word for "desert." For the average Russian it contains a synthesis of the words: prayer, penance, mortification, solitude, and silence.

As Catherine put it:

The poustinia is an entry into the desert, a lonely place... a silent place where one can lift the two arms of prayer and penance to God in atonement, intercession, reparation, for one's sins and those of one's brothers.

The *poustinia* experience cleanses and strengthens the soul, clarifies the mind's grasp of the supernatural, and reawakens fervor in the soul. It is a springboard for songs of love and joy offered to God.

When I was in Combermere, I made my first *poustinia*. At first I felt a strange discomfort in being alone in total silence. At the end of the twenty-four hours, I felt refreshed and fortified.

I felt touched by God in some way, and was absolutely clear about my purpose and direction.

Consider making a poustinia of your own. You don't have to go to a cabin in the woods to do it. Perhaps you could escape to a retreat house, or a guesthouse, or any private place with no TV. Shut out the noise of the world, and rest yourself in a disposition of unstructured prayer and fasting. They recommend that you take only a loaf of bread and a jug of water. Then enter the world of silence. The experience will renew your spirit.

In 1978, I invited Catherine to be a guest on my television show, "Christopher Closeup." She accepted, and came to New York City. Before the cameras began rolling, I suggested that she keep her answers short, knowing that she could go on and on at times. To my amazement she took it literally, and began giving me one-word answers. The interview at first went something like this:

"You wrote a book entitled The Gospel Without Compromise. *Do you think there are many people in the world who actually live the Gospel without compromise?"*
"NO."

"Why did you choose Combermere, Ontario as the place to begin your apostolate?"
"GOD."

I had to smile and stop the taping. I told her she could elaborate a bit more on her answers, which she did, and from then on everything was fine.

The following are some edited excerpts from that interview, which was conducted by myself and Jeanne Glynn:

JG: What does *Poustinia* mean?

CD: *Poustinia* is the desert experience. Of course, you can live alone with God in the midst of work. I have to lecture, but that doesn't stop me from praying, since it's my duty to live in God even if I have to lecture. I lecture, but my heart is with God, and I have to tell Him: I am with you.

This is the way I have it figured out: If you go to the desert to pray, you still live in this world to learn *Sobornost* – unity – the unity of God and man. And then comes the trial, when God touches you on the shoulder and says: *Come on, you're ready to preach the Gospel to others.*

JC: How does one make a *poustinia*?

CD: A *poustinia* is a little cabin in which you go to pray for a day or so. We have about fifteen of them. There is a cross in it, like you're supposed to hang on that cross with Jesus. There is a mat on the floor for you to lie on, and there is a writing table. You take with you a loaf of bread, and some water. You can take coffee or tea if you like. They go into the cabin with water, bread and the Gospel. That's about it. They go and they pray, but it has to be very, very free. There has to be no tension, nothing to do.

We tell them, if you want to sleep, sleep. If you want to walk around the place, go ahead and walk. Be absolutely free. God will come to you in a certain way, at a certain time. And those who have been to the *poustinia* four or five times have experienced God. Later, slowly, they come and they say: *I think I am beginning to meet God in this desert of silence.*

JC: For some of our listeners who might be interested in making their own private *poustinia*, is there anything you could advise them?

CD: It's so simple. When I was a child and I failed an examination, my father said: "Don't get excited. Go to the *poustinia* and think it over." He meant a little room or even a little corner. So I used to go; and this was done by many Russians. So you have to go into a corner. You have to find a place, if you really want to make a *poustinia*, where you can meet God and clear out all the mess that is in your heart.

JC: How long a period of time would you suggest?

CD: I would suggest for a Western person, one day a week is the most that they can do. Two days a month is okay. After that they develop the hunger for God. The hunger for God gets very great. Then they do one a week, two a week, three a week.

JG: Baroness, what can be done to alleviate the loneliness that many of us feel? Is it talking it out to someone, or listening to someone?

CD: That's it: listening. Listening with love. You don't have to be a psychiatrist, a psychologist, or a consultant, getting 49 dollars for half an hour. No. Listen because you love this person.

JG: What gives you hope?

CD: Faith.

JG: And where does that faith come from?

CD: That faith comes first from Baptism, and secondly from falling in love with God. Thirdly, from my family. Fourthly, from my environment. The Russian environment of older days. Right here. It's very strong in me. But I can give it to you; it's all yours for the asking.

Hope does not disappoint us,
because God's love
has been poured into our hearts
through the Holy Spirit
that has been given to us.

Romans 5:5

7

LEON-JOSEF CARDINAL SUENENS

Since we are all baptized, we are baptized in water, and in the Holy Spirit. So the Holy Spirit is there in us as the power of God, as the light of God. just as the sun gives radiance all over the world, so too the Holy Spirit always gives us insights, powers, and gifts. The word "charisma" is used more specifically to indicate certain visible manifestations of the Spirit acting in the world. However, the most important gifts of the Spirit are faith, hope and love. But we don't call them charismas, because the idea of charisma is linked with visible manifestations of the Spirit. So I think we should just be very grateful to the Lord essentially for His gifts of faith, hope and charity, as we open ourselves to follow his inspiration.

Leon-Josef Suenens, pronounced 'Soon-uns', was a young priest in the 1940's when he was taken hostage by the Nazis in occupied Belgium. His execution was averted in the nick of time by the Allied liberation. He gave me a brief description of his life in an interview I did with him in 1980:

I was born in Brussels on July 16, 1904. My life was stamped at an early date by the death of my father when I was not quite four years old. I was an only son.

My mother, who was deeply religious, courageously assumed the burdens of widowhood and poverty. It is due to her strong faith that I was able to learn the art of living day by day, a truly Christian life.

At seventeen, I knocked at the door of the Malines Seminary. To my great surprise my bishop, the great and illustrious Cardinal Mercier, sent me to study in Rome. This resulted in a close bond with him, which developed over the years through correspondence and regular visits. It is through him that I learned to appreciate the Church's universal dimension, and the Church's call to ecumenism.

I spent seven years in Rome, which was a great joy for me. And later, when the Council started I felt very much at ease in Rome, having been there so long. I was comfortable with the Italian language. After that I returned to Belgium, and became professor of philosophy at the University of Louvain for ten years, then serving as the vice rector for an additional five years. That was all during World War II.

Later I was made an auxiliary bishop, and I selected as my motto "In Spiritu Sancto" (In the Holy Spirit). My shield contained a silver dove soaring in a blue background, a symbol of Mary. This image captured the essence of my whole life, which I saw as one lived in deep union with Mary. I wanted to imitate her "Fiat," which means her "Yes" to the Holy Spirit's invitation to give birth to His Son. I wanted the grace and power of the Holy Spirit to lead me in my life. On the ecclesial level, the image on my shield was also an expression of my wish to serve a Church that transcended the administrative and canonical institution, a Church that was also open to the unforeseen, and therefore to the surprises of the Holy Spirit. And such surprises were not lacking.

In 1961 Pope John XXIII made me an Archbishop, and when he decided to convoke the Second Vatican Council, he made

*me a Cardinal, appointing me as one of the Council's four
moderators.*

Cardinal Suenens was amazed by his own rise to power. He
never sought it, but in God's providence, it always came to him.
He is not yet up for canonization, but I think he will be.
He produced such a rich spiritual legacy. In spite of his fame
and prominence in the Church, the Cardinal always remained
a modest man.

He once told me about the effect his father's death had on
him.

*My father's death occurred when I was three. It showed
me how short life can be. I understood with total clarity at
that early age, that even if one lived to be a hundred, it is
essential to live one's life with eternity in mind. This idea
became the natural basis of my vocation, which took the
form of a desire to prepare men and women for their final
and everlasting destiny.*

I was with Cardinal Suenens when my father died in 1993.

I was traveling in Ireland with him when we received the
news that my Dad, who was retired and living in Florida, passed
away. He had suffered a massive stroke two months before his
86th birthday. I was the director of The Christophers at the time,
living in New York City, and flew down immediately to be at his
side. When I arrived at Holy Cross Hospital in Fort Lauderdale,
Dad was in a deep coma. There was nothing I could do but sit
helplessly by his side for the next two weeks.

However, I had made an appointment to be with Cardinal
Suenens that next week, and I was torn about leaving my Dad.
Should I cancel the trip or not? What if he lasted another few
months in this condition? My meeting with Suenens was to be-

gin in Ireland, where representatives from Veritas, a publishing house in Dublin, were promoting his newest book, *Memories and Hopes*. The Cardinal had asked me to tape a TV interview with him for viewing in English-speaking countries.

I didn't want to leave Florida, but the Cardinal phoned and encouraged me to come, trusting my Dad to God's will. So I decided to take the chance and go to Ireland, with the idea of returning immediately after I finished the taping; and off I went.

The day we finished the taping word came that my Dad had died. The Cardinal consoled me, and that day he and I concelebrated a private Mass for my father's happy repose. As I flew back across the ocean, I had many memories of the fun I had with my father as I was growing up. One such memory is worth noting.

My Dad and I used to perform a little acrobatic trick, which gave my mother fits. She was a saint in her own right, and never felt comfortable when my Dad lifted me high above his head and balanced me on his hand. He would walk me around, and I was literally ten feet tall.

I was about three at the time when Dad taught me to step on to his hand, which he would put on the floor. Then he would take my two hands in his other hand, and slowly lift me up over his head. He had me stiffen my body, so that when I felt secure enough, he would gently let go of my hands, and raise me up slowly on his right hand. He would then walk me around in a balancing act that had everybody worried. Somehow I felt perfectly secure because I knew he wouldn't drop me. Here's why!

We had a plan. He made me promise that if I lost balance I would know enough to lean forward, and he would see to it that I fell across his other arm. We practiced the art of falling forward where I would grab his left arm, and then swing gently down to the ground. It worked every time. I gained more and more confidence until I had no fear whatsoever.

I mention this little story because my father, without knowing it, taught me about trust. I knew I could put my trust in him. I knew he would never drop me. It was a wonderful preparation for my future relationship with God the Father.

Instinctively, I was taught to trust God, as I did my own father, and to this day I am so grateful to my Dad for teaching me such a valuable lesson.

My father died in Holy Cross Hospital in Fort Lauderdale, Florida. When I arrived there, I made arrangements to ship his body up to Jackson Heights, New York, where I had grown up in the parish of St. Joan of Arc.

My Christopher Closeup interview with Cardinal Suenens, was taped in 1988 at HBO Studios in New York City. Here is the transcript of that conversation.

JC: Your work carries you all over the world and I wonder, Cardinal, since you have traveled so widely and seen many countries, how do you connect with people of different races and nationalities? You speak six languages fluently, how do you find the flexibility to move about from one culture to another?

CS: People are essentially the same everywhere. This is my deep conviction. The philosophers raise the same questions for humans everywhere. What's the meaning of life? What's the meaning of suffering? Where are we going after death? And so on. That's the eternal dimension of human life. Everywhere you go, the context of life may be changed, but basically we all have the same human nature.

The basic truth is that Christ is the answer to mankind's needs. Because of this commonality, I feel at ease everywhere I go in the world, especially in the United States. That is the main reason why I came back here. It's been 15 years since my last trip. I feel an openness and a frankness here, which makes things very comfortable. I like your way of being straightforward, and calling a spade a spade. I have the impression that in America there is an absence of intrigue and complications. I think Americans are straightforward in their manner. That is my general impression.

JC: For the most part I think that's true. Tell me, as a churchman who has been involved with television from very early days. How did that come about? What potential did you see in television?

CS: The potential is enormous in the sense that on TV you are the teacher of all those who are looking at you, listening to you. Even if you have no intention of teaching something, the influence is immense because you can present things in different ways. I sense this especially when religious news is given. The temptation is always to reduce it to something sensational. It's very difficult to speak about things in depth on TV. When some religious aspect is shown on television very often it's just a superficial report.

As a result the viewer sees the Church interpreted through the vantage point of the secular media. For instance, when they report on the Church and are speaking about a big event, something rather extraordinary, of course we realize that it is not the secular reporter's role to speak about the supernatural essentials beneath the surface; like the mystery of Christ living in the Church, and the role of the Spirit in the Church. All that is hidden from view, but needs to be mentioned.

It is always important to see how the Holy Spirit is working within the reality of the Church, and inside our own souls. So, my feeling is that when you see the Holy Spirit at work in our life, you must try to allow the Spirit to lead you. You know the saying, we cannot direct the wind, but we can adjust our sails.

That is what I meant when I chose *"In Spiritu Sancto," "In the Holy Spirit,"* as my episcopal motto.

JC: Please explain that further.

CS: I often read about the tension between say the invisible aspect of the prophetic Church and the institutional Church. There is no such thing as two Churches. There is only one reality with two dimensions. There is the charismatic or the invisible Church, and then also there is the visible structure. But the reality is that there is only one Church, one totality. As a bishop, it is always my intention to ask the Lord to help me follow where the Holy Spirit is leading me.

For instance, I once saw the work of the Holy Spirit coming to us from Ireland. A wind was blowing, showing me the work of God in the Legion of Mary. I saw something in that pastoral initiative, and felt that here was something new. At that time, the lay apostolate was new, and so too was this kind of devotion to Mary, which had evangelization as its aim. This was something new. Mary was consecrated to the Holy Spirit from the beginning. The Spirit first came to her at the Annunciation, and Jesus came to life in her. That was an early sign of the movement of the Spirit. Centuries later came the Second Vatican Council, which was not only a breeze, but also a mighty wind coming from the Holy Spirit.

John XXIII asked the bishops of the world to come together to begin a "New Pentecost," and to start praying the way the Apostles and Mary prayed for guidance in the Upper Room on that first Pentecost.

Pope John deliberately opened the Council on the Feast of the Motherhood of Mary, October 11, 1962, and I immediately felt I was on the same wavelength with him. From this was born a close collaboration regarding the Council preparation, and its first session.

At the end of this first session, and a few weeks before he died, Pope John XXIII entrusted me with the mission of presenting the new Encyclical, *Pacem in Terris,* to the United Nations in

New York. This, for him, was like a spiritual testament addressed not only to Christians, but to all people of good will.

This document received an astounding welcome in the world. It was a great joy for me to offer a commentary on it to the United Nations assembly. This was one of the outstanding events of my life. I offered U Thant, who was the U.N. Secretary General at the time, a copy of it, with an autographed dedication by John XXIII.

The Holy Father died on Pentecost Monday, in June 1963. As a sign of paternal affection, he bequeathed me the stole he had worn at the opening of the Council.

Paul VI succeeded John XXIII and asked me to make the solemn speech of homage to his memory at the opening of the second session of the Council in October 1963. Then Paul VI re-appointed me as one of the four Council moderators, and I was plunged into the very heart of its proceedings.

JC: As one of the four moderators of the Second Vatican Council, and as the Archbishop of Brussels you have been involved with the official visible Church a great deal, but you mentioned the other dimension of the Church, the invisible or charismatic one, which lives inside the institutional Church. Obviously you have been prominent in both dimensions of the Church. When Pope Paul VI appointed you to be the leader of the Catholic Charismatic Movement worldwide, how did you react?

CS: Well, of course I was delighted. First Paul VI appointed me the head of the Charismatics, then his successor, John Paul II, reappointed me after Pope Paul's death. The idea was to unite the invisible Church and the visible. This is at the heart of the continuity of the Incarnation. The Church is the visible presence of the mystery of Christ beneath the surface. It is there that the Holy Spirit is working. Everyone sees the visible side. I think we have to do a better job of bringing the two together.

So the Vatican Council stressed a bit more the visible side, because we needed to make some changes, for instance in collegiality, involving the creation of synods and councils, and so on. Here the emphasis at the Council was obviously the visible side of the Church, but this is not the most profound side. So then Pope Paul VI said that the Second Vatican Council must now be carried forward, and he wanted to stress more the mysterious Christological side. This is the dimension which shows forth the Holy Spirit working among us.

For me, in this position as papal representative to the Charismatics, I serve the same Church, but now I stress more the spiritual side, the Charismatic side if you like. Since both Popes, Paul VI and also Pope John Paul II asked me to oversee the development of the Charismatic Renewal, I have the task of seeing to its full integration into the Church. And that's the reason why I'm so interested in the Charismatic Movement.

JC: Why is it called a movement?

CS: The word charismatic refers to the gifts of the Spirit. If I had to make a choice, I would not have named it the Charismatic Movement, because it's not strictly speaking a movement. I would rather call it a motion of the Spirit. If you speak about it as a movement, that's good too, but it's a movement which in the end is supposed to disappear. Let me explain… Today the liturgy is alive again because of the Liturgical Movement of the past thirty years, but now there is no longer a reason for the Liturgical Movement. It has done its job as a reform movement.

JC: How would you apply this idea to the Ecumenical Movement?

CS: Today, the visible unity of all the Christian Churches is being restored slowly. One day there will be no reason to call it the Ecumenical Movement. We will all be one. In the same way my dream is that the Charismatic Movement, as a movement, will disappear because its aim is that each of us, every Christian on earth will be renewed in his or her faith as one People of God. That's the hope.

When we stress the word charismatic, we are referring especially to the gifts of the Spirit. But the essence of the Spirit is more important than the gifts. So I prefer to speak of it as the renewal in the Spirit. It is a new awareness of what the presence of the Spirit means for you in your own being, in your own soul, and in the life of the Church, and also in the life of the world. That's for me the vision of what the Church is in the depth of its being. l don't like to say this person is a Charismatic Christian, or this person is not a Charismatic Christian, because every Christian is charismatic in the sense that we all receive the gifts of the Spirit. Otherwise he or she is not Christian. In the same way you might say this person is baptized or this one is not baptized.

JC: Please elaborate further on the gifts of the Spirit.

CS: Each gift makes for a greater whole, it builds up the mystical Body of Christ. Nobody is in possession of all the gifts. St. Paul said, "One is a teacher, another has a gift for administration, another for the healing ministry..." and so on. That's the complementarity of the Christian Church, the Body of Christ. Because of this, I think what we are striving for, especially since Vatican II, is harmony. We need these gifts as an expression of complementarity. Working together is what the Lord is asking us to do.

JC: What do you think is the future of the Ecumenical Movement?

CS: I wrote a book called *Ecumenism and Charismatic Renewal: Theological and Pastoral Orientations* as a sort of clarification of what the charismatic renewal was and really should be, giving a sort of theological vision of the meaning of charismatic renewal. Then I wrote a follow-up book to show how the charismatic renewal could be an instrument for a new approach to true ecumenism. My goal is to bring people together in that communion in the Holy Spirit, across different denominations. The Christian denominations have a common ground. They need to meet and love each other... I think this is a step towards visible unity. If ecumenism remains only on the level of a dialogue between theologians, then it remains above the heads of people. It has to be done by all. It's going on now on the personal level and going on very well. But if you really wish that Christians of all denominations should be really involved praying for union, we have to stress that aspect in daily life. We are already one in the Spirit in an invisible way, now we must make it visible.

JC: Cardinal, at the heart of the Charismatic Movement and at the heart of the mystery of the Church is Jesus Christ. Tell us a little about the Charismatic Movement and then speak a little about Jesus and what He means to you.

CS: He means everything. He is the fundamental answer to life, the reason for living... essentially the reason for our hope and the reason to remain joyful at the end of my life. I am now nearly 75. I'm at a point where I see Christ coming. I am waiting for Christ. This is the fullness of the meaning of life. He is really my reason to enjoy the future, my reason to be grateful for the past. He called me to my vocation. I felt it and I experienced it as a loving presence of the Lord all through my life. And so the past, the present and the future are filled by His presence, by His meaning. He gives meaning to my life, to every moment of my life. So really when I say He is all for me, it is really true.

As for the renewal, it gave new life to my faith. I saw how some Christians live, taking the Acts of the Apostles at its word, and this led me to question the depth and the genuineness of my own faith. As a result I found I believed in the action of the

Spirit, but in a limited sphere; in me the Spirit could not call forth from the pipe organ all the melodies possible. Some of the pipes did not function because they had not been used... I saw in the renewal a spiritual youth as it were, a more tangible hope, and the joy of seeing impossible things become possible... the surest sign of the renewal's authenticity rests in its Christology.

In proclaiming "Jesus is Lord," the charismatics affirm that Jesus is the Son of God in a unique manner, and it thus distinguishes itself from countless "back to Jesus" movements which often present us with a purely human Jesus. I am discovering that God is nearer than I thought, that a charism is a manifestation of His glorious love, the love He feels for me and wishes to reveal through me. I found too I did not realize Our Lord's promise that His disciples would "do greater works than He because He was going to the Father and would send His Spirit" (John 14:12).

I also learned that my prayer life was too individualistic. The presence of others close to me on these occasions of murmuring spontaneous prayers, at first, annoyed me. It took some time to learn that prayer can be deeply personal and yet part of a "symphony." I was struck by the freedom with which people expressed themselves in prayer, even in an exterior symbolic way. Some lifted up their hands from time to time. So habituated are we – and I especially – to control our emotions and conceal anything that might reveal what is going on inside us. Timidity, human respect, inhibitions, the education we have received: all this conditions us to assume a mask of reserve. We are ready to pray with our soul, but not with our body. We have to respect the differences among us: "There are many rooms in my Father's house" (John 14:2) – but the foundation of the house is one.

JC: Cardinal, in today's very confusing world, many people struggle with their Christianity, with their relationship with the Lord. What do you have to say to someone like that?

CS: Well of course it depends on different situations, where they are in their level of faith, but normally we should start with conversion. Saying "no" to certain things we know to be against evangelical values like renouncing bad habits, which might be sinful. There is a sort of rupture between what the world considers to be of true value, and what Jesus taught as being of value. I'm thinking about drugs, egotism and all that. So we should first experience a sort of emptying. If you wish to be filled with the Spirit of the Lord you must first be empty, at least to the extent of being open to the Lord. And then once that's done, and almost at the same time, because you do not do that first and then go to the second stage, all of it is done at the same time, then I think it's essential to pray. You say, "Lord if You are there, if You exist, help me to see You, help me to listen to You." And if you really enter that silence you will hear the voice of the Lord speaking. One of the essential ways of finding meaning to life is creating a zone of silence, a long moment of silence. So I recommend going on a retreat, and there listen carefully at what the Lord is saying to you. Try to meet and mingle with Christians who are really living Christianity. Nothing is stronger than to see how Christians, who are really Christians, live their lives. I think that's one of the ways of living the Gospel.

JC: You mentioned "renouncing sin." The word "sin" has lost some of its punch these days. A lot of people don't even consider it a reality. What do you say about that?

CS: The world is becoming profoundly de-christianized. We are witnessing a de-sacralization of love and human life. In the name of free love, people are claiming the right to complete sexual freedom – which is spreading like an epidemic among the young and breaking up many homes.

As for respect for human life, the right to abortion which is being claimed, is from its inception, a sinister denial of life.

There is no end to the signs of moral disarray in family, social and political life.

As for the notion of "sin," yes, the term has disappeared from our vocabulary, so that even mentioning it is seen as an anachronism.

Faced with all this, how can Christians remain silent in this pluralistic world of ours? They are asked to avoid any kind of statement, which others see as an assault on freedom – while in the meantime the drug sub-culture is increasing its devastation among Christian ranks.

Against this dark background, however, signs of spiritual renewal stand out like rays of light.

I am thinking of:

- Christians gathered in "cells" or pastoral teams, ready to undertake the revitalization of a parish;
- diocesan councils contributing to the gradual renewal of the Church;
- new communities seeking to live a totally Christian life within the world;
- many initiatives in support of those who are poor materially and spiritually;
- retreats and spiritual weekends taking place everywhere.
- the birth, or rebirth, of contemplative orders;
- the healthy reaction of young people forming groups to safeguard the basic values of all civilization.

These give us hope for the "New Evangelization." But if this spirit is to find its wings, there is one condition: the "New Evangelization" must be inspired by the "First Evangelization," that which was born at Pentecost in the Jerusalem Cenacle.

There is need to return to this fountainhead of all evangelization; there is need to recall Jesus' promise to His apostles when He was about to leave them: "You will be given power, that of the Holy Spirit which will come down upon you. You will then be My witnesses in Jerusalem... even to the ends of the earth" (Acts 1:8).

Those who have lived, and still live, this original grace of renewal called "Baptism of the Spirit," or the new outpouring of the Spirit, have testified that they had "encountered" the Lord in a life-transforming spiritual experience – an experience comparable to a new conversion.

Their testimony has been heard, but their message, which is addressed to us all, has passed unnoticed. Instead, attention has been focused on the marginal aspects of renewal, such as the extraordinary gifts, like speaking in tongues. As a result we have not seen the forest for the trees. In short, the grace of renewal has not been given a chance to flourish. It is like the seed that fell on stony ground in the Gospel story.

The future will tell whether the people of God will open up one day to welcome the renewal in the Spirit to the limit of its depth and breadth.

JC: What do you mean by the term "people of God"?

CS: Since God created the world it follows that every human being is a member of that creation. The people of God include all those created by God. If I use the word in a more strict sense, I would first say they are the people of the new covenant, all those who follow Jesus Christ as Lord, those who enter in the full intimacy with the Lord. To be united with the Lord means that they are called to serve their neighbor in a more profound way.

We can all serve our neighbor, just out of human love. But if we love somebody with the heart of God Himself, that love is deeper. So that is our invitation and calling. The people of God are invited to be nearer to God and nearer to neighbors. Nearer to God in order to be nearer to people.

So that's what the expression "people of God" means, in that context.

In Vatican Council II we defined the term to apply primarily to members of the Catholic Church, and then to all the baptized Christians, and lastly to everyone else, i.e. in the broadest sense, all human beings are God's people.

JC: Mother Teresa of Calcutta has had a tremendous impact on the world. As a matter of fact, recently she was on the cover of *Time* magazine. They did an article on living saints. Her life makes a statement, which I think gives us a beautiful example of carrying Christ in the world. She said something which I think was profound and I'd be interested in your comment on it. She said that expressing the love of the Lord should begin at home, in the family, with your own mother, father, sisters and brothers. If you can do that well, then you should reach out to others in need. Please comment on that.

CS: Well, she's a living example of what true Christian love means, what she says is very striking. She said somewhere that we are not social workers. We are meant to be contemplatives. Going to the poor because we see Christ in the poor. She also said that what she was doing for the poor was merely a continuity of her Eucharistic celebration in the morning. Just as Jesus is there in the Eucharist each day, He is also present in the poor. It is a way of seeing people, a continuation of her prayer life in the service of others.

JC: Seeing the face of Christ in one's neighbor, brings about a continual union with Christ.

CS: Union with Christ, yes. I think that's an important thing to stress. There is some sort of an artificial division today between what some call Charismatic Christians and what others call social action Christians, as though they were separate divisions, as if you had to make a choice between the two. No, the logic of prayer, of contemplation, is that the social action apostolate flows from prayer and the logic for a Christian apostolate is that it should be rooted in prayer. That's the reason why I will publish in a few weeks a book, *Renewal and Social Commitment*, to show that the two are really one, and that we have to find our way to unite them.

JC: The Christophers have been teaching this theme for years. The idea that it's not enough to have a private prayer life. Your prayer life should blossom and become so real that the love of God flows through to those in need.

CS: I think at The Christophers you have a gift. I have received every month, your little News Notes, those little pamphlets you send out to the world. I must say I appreciate them very much. You have a gift of saying important ideas in a nutshell, and at the same time of being very practical. I think that's a wonderful American gift.

JC: Cardinal Suenens we started this interview talking about hope, now let us end on that theme. Would you say a word about hope for our audience?

CS: Well, once you believe that God is love, and since we know that love is at the beginning of everything, we also know that God will be at the end of everything. We don't know all that will be in between, but we do know that we started from the heart of a loving Father, and at the end of our story the Father will be receiving us with open arms. Just reread the story of the Prodigal Son, and focus not on the son's sins but on the father's love. He is there waiting to receive the sinner, and we are all sinners.

JC: Tell us a little bit about your idea of heaven.

CS: I believe heaven is not a place of final retirement: I imagine that there we will be more active than ever, but in a manner that is inconceivable on earth.

In any event, as soon as the Lord will be so good as to let me in, I would like to meet St. Paul, the Master of the Apostolate, and ask him to inspire those in charge of our seminaries and novitiates to train our seminarians in the art of direct evangelization. This will take practical change in the curriculum so that those who, tomorrow, will be charged with promoting the "New Evangelization" may learn how to teach lay people their co-responsibility with them in the common task of Gospel-preaching.

Not only would I ask St. Paul to help the Church in initiating direct evangelization, but also for help in teaching people to live Christianity as adults, starting out with "Baptism in the Spirit and Fire." We need to take seriously, in the programs of our seminaries and novitiates, the advice St. Paul gave the Corinthians about the wisdom of the world and the folly of the cross (1 Corinthians 1:19-25).

We are yet to discover the deepest sense of the mystery of God's love and to experience this inexpressible love of His in a personal way.

If only we could make people understand that faith is not something to be known, but something to be lived, that the conversion of the heart opens the door to knowledge, and that the last word is "love," which is the very definition of God.

As I stand waiting for my entrance into heaven, the closer I am to death, the more I perceive how my inner self is growing in joy and hope.

JC: Thank you Cardinal Suenens for this wonderful visit.

From Cardinal Suenens I learned the importance of trusting the Holy Spirit. This man of such deep faith, had a childlike humility when it came to the majesty of God. He realized that he is nothing, and that God is all. This is a characteristic that all the saints possess.

Owe no person anything
Except to love one another;
For whoever loves his neighbor
Has fulfilled the law.

Romans 13:8

8

ARCHBISHOP JOSEPH M. RAYA

God is not an old bachelor in the sky. God is relationship!
God is Trinity! The God of our Christian revelation is
a social life, and infinite superabundance of life... He is
the fullness of communion and thereby is the source of all
communion.

Archbishop Joseph M. Raya became the bishop of the area where Jesus grew up, the land of Akko-Haifa-Nazareth and all of Galilee. He was born in Zahle, Lebanon on August 15, 1916, the Feast of the Assumption, and was nurtured as a child by the Melkite Byzantine tradition.

After primary studies in Paris, and seminary studies with the White Fathers in Jerusalem, he was ordained to the priesthood on July 20, 1941, and was later assigned to teach history and philosophy at St. Anne's Minor Seminary in Zahle. Then he was appointed by his Patriarch to serve as superintendent of schools in Cairo, Egypt; and later as director of the Patriarchal College there.

I knew him as a simple priest when he was assigned in the Diocese of Paterson, New Jersey. After he became an archbishop, he invited me and some mutual friends to come as his guests in the Holy Land for a week. I wrote an article about that visit, which I have included below, to give you my early impressions of him as he began his new assignment.

In a land so permeated with a sense of the holy, the sad fact is that hatred is thriving between Arabs and Jews. In the midst of this hatred, one prophetic voice is speaking forthrightly to both sides – Archbishop Joseph Raya, bishop of Akko, Haifa, Nazareth and all Galilee.

Born in Lebanon, he was an Arab through and through, a man of extraordinary power and authenticity. To understand his influence, one must first realize that Arabs live in a patriarchal society. Among the Arab-speaking citizens of Israel, there are Christians, Moslems, and Druze. The vast majority of the Christian Arabs are Melkite Catholics, in union with Rome, and under the authority of Archbishop Raya.

The non-Christian Arabs have no comparable patriarch, which puts them at a distinct disadvantage both politically and psychologically. Consequently they turn to Archbishop Raya, the most important Arab in the country, as their spokesman. What impressed me most about him was his absolute and total commitment to the Gospel of Jesus Christ. When he first arrived, he gave a speech on television calling upon all the Arab people to put down their hatred for the Jews, and to follow the teaching of Christ by striving for brotherhood with them.

In the next breath, he challenged the Israeli government to rectify the injustices done to the Arab refugees, to return their lands, and to provide shelter for the homeless among them.

Each side was stung by his reproach. Passions ride high in this country of deadly enemies. Neither side was pleased with his attitude.

It is one thing to make a speech and then go into hiding, but Archbishop Raya has been speaking continually since he arrived. I was with him in a tiny village where many Arab refugees had migrated years before. They filled every corner of the available shelter to the point of bursting. These people have been driven from their land, and have been virtually homeless since 1948, so they were in no mood for a brotherhood talk from anyone.

But the archbishop in his full regalia, commanded them to stop hating the Jews, and to purge their hearts of hatred and contention. He said this would only breed more misery and suffering.

At the closing session of the Israeli parliament he scolded the Jewish officials, speaking in French, Arabic, and English so that everyone would understand. He lamented the fact that the Jews have done to the Arabs some of the very same things they themselves suffered in their own history of persecution.

It was quite a thing to see a living prophet in action, challenging the inflamed passions of ancient enemies with the Gospel of Jesus Christ.

Christ is alive and well in Galilee.

Father Raya served earlier in his priesthood at St. Anne's Melkite Church in Paterson, New Jersey. When he was there, he and José de Vinck collaborated in publishing a beautiful English translation of the *Byzantine Missal*.

José and I had written a book together entitled *The Challenge of Love* so it was he who introduced me to Raya.

We had a lot in common. We were both interested in the civil rights movement. He made the black community's struggle for freedom and dignity his own, and this no doubt led to his transfer from Paterson, New Jersey to a Melkite parish in Birmingham, Alabama.

In that highly tense interracial setting, he invited African-Americans to attend his all-white church. In Birmingham that was a no-no. He became a friend of Martin Luther King, Jr. whose Baptist Church was only a few blocks away from his own. Raya even marched at the side of King in the protest movement.

In 1965 my life strangely converged with the lives of Father Raya and Doctor Martin Luther King, Jr. I came down to join Dr. King's march in Selma. It involved the historic struggle to register black voters in the South. The black population in Alabama had been virtually denied the right to vote because of many devious registration policies used by the white majority to keep them from the polls.

The "Bloody Sunday Incident," on March 7, 1965, triggered off an incident which received national coverage. I was shocked watching the news on television one night when Alabama policemen brutally beat a group of black protesters.

Six hundred marchers were on their way to Montgomery to protest voting rights abuses, but before they got underway they were clubbed and tear-gassed by the Alabama state troopers. They were crossing the Edmund Pettus Bridge when the attacks began.

My heart was sickened by the shameless display of raw power used against unarmed American citizens. They had been marching peacefully, expressing their first amendment right to free speech when the violent confrontation began. It included the use of high-powered water hoses on men, women and children. I was sitting in my rectory in Wayne, New Jersey, watching in disbelief.

Two days later another incident occurred. Three Protestant clergymen, who had gone to Selma to express their solidarity with the protesters, were walking past the Silver Moon Café, when a group of white racists came out with clubs, and beat them mercilessly. One of the blows landed so heavily on the skull of the Rev. James J. Reeb, a Boston Unitarian minister, that he was taken to Birmingham's University Hospital where he died without recovering consciousness. News of the incident inflamed the entire nation.

Msgr. Jack Eagan of Chicago, one of the nation's leading Catholic social activists, called me, asking that I come to Selma with a delegation to help express Catholic outrage and solidarity against those who did the killing. We suspected that it was the work of the Ku Klux Klan.

The reason Jack called me was because I was the founder of the Paterson Diocesan Catholic Interracial Council at the time. I had no trouble getting Bishop James Navagh, my boss, to give me permission to take two others to Selma. I chose Father John Simonet and a layman named Jim Lamb to accompany me.

Upon arriving we found out that Alabama's Governor George C. Wallace had given the order to prevent any marchers from leaving Selma. He didn't want them reaching the State Capitol in Montgomery. This meant that we were all forced to remain in a closed compound in Selma.

A police guard, led by the public safety commissioner Eugene "Bull" Connor kept us contained, claiming that he was protecting us from possible attacks by the rednecks. He was probably right. There were some very angry men circling around us, in cars, yelling foul and hateful words.

During those four days of containment, we all prayed with Dr. King in Brown Chapel. We listened as he explained his policy of nonviolent persuasion. He rejected all violent resistance to these injustices, in the manner of Gandhi. Jesus Christ inspired all those who believe in non-violence.

King seized the moment, and used the media to demand national legislation to protect the rights of voters all through the South.

Father Raya and I and many others cheered him on, as did millions of TV viewers. The pressure was put firmly on Gov. George Wallace to do something. Unfortunately John Simonet,

Jim Lamb and I had to return home before the march was allowed to proceed. We left a few days before Wallace caved in on March 21, 1965. The protesters began their march to Montgomery, and by that time 25,000 protesters had assembled. When the marchers finally arrived at the steps of the Alabama State Capitol, Dr. King addressed a national audience with these memorable words:

How long will it take? Not long, because no lie can live forever, and because the arm of the moral universe is long, but it always bends toward justice.

Those words were prophetic because almost within hours, President Lyndon Johnson responded by pushing new legislations through Congress in record time. The right to register and vote was finally guaranteed, and the rest is history.

In that entire experience with Dr. Martin Luther King, Jr. and Father Raya, I saw the Holy Spirit working through them and through the People of God. It taught me that the Holy Spirit is alive and well, working behind the scenes, and beyond the borders of the Catholic Church. We are all one people.

I wish I could have gotten closer to Dr. King to interview him, but that was not to be. Father Raya later told us a story about his abduction one night a few weeks after the march. Three men wearing white hoods dragged him from his rectory in Birmingham, and beat him mercilessly. They called him a nigger lover, and he shouted back, "Yes I am a nigger lover, and I am a Ku Klux Klan lover too." When they finished with him they left him on the road and disappeared into the night.

Father Joseph Raya's courage did not go unnoticed by Church authorities. In 1967, the Holy Synod of the Melkite Church appointed him to be the next Archbishop of Akka, Haifa, Nazareth and all of Galilee. His episcopal consecration took place in Birmingham, Alabama on October 20, 1968.

Once he was settled into his new home in Haifa, Israel, he invited me and the de Vincks to come for a week. On that visit, he gave us a royal tour of the Holy Land.

We watched Archbishop Raya firsthand carrying on valiantly in his new assignment. Committed as he was to the Gospel, he presented his vision of how things should be. It was a vision of brotherly love, which encompassed people of all races. Consequently he spoke out without fear. At times, the very people he was trying to help turned against him.

He had a prophetic gift. I had never seen a prophet up close and personal, but here was Father Raya calling for love and forgiveness in a land filled with hatred. The storms he fomented by his outspoken idealism, eventually led to his persecution. Finally he had to resign. In 1974 it came to a head over a matter that had to do with the redistribution of real estate to the Palestinians living in his area. It is too complicated to explain, but Raya was on the side of the angels.

Returning home to North America, he took up permanent residence at Madonna House in Combermere, Ontario. From the beginning, Catherine Doherty recognized in him a unique presence. He helped her to bring her vision of *"a Church that breathed with the two lungs,"* into reality. As she put it, both the Eastern Church, which had the Byzantine liturgy, and the Church of Rome, which has the Latin Rite are two parts of the beautiful Body of Christ.

The two Rites were united at Madonna House, not merged. Archbishop Joseph Raya's readiness to present the Byzantine liturgy from time to time gave everyone a taste of the richness of another tradition. He not only celebrated the Byzantine liturgy; he lived and breathed it with his whole being. He always seemed to exude a sense of God's love.

In 1983 he was ordered by his superiors to renew his theological studies. As a result he attended some Melkite seminaries and monasteries to study further the Byzantine traditions.

Afterward he wrote an entire theological curriculum in Arabic, called *Byzantine Theology*. This treatise served students in Lebanon, Israel, Egypt and Syria. He also served as president of the commission working for the establishment of a Melkite eparchy in the United States.

A man of extraordinary inner freedom and spontaneity, Archbishop Joseph stepped outside the usual conventions of spirituality, and set people on fire with his vision that the beauty of God is reflected in every human face. One young person who admired him put it this way, *"He sees beyond the physical reality. He sees the glorious potential in every person. His love makes people feel beautiful."*

Archbishop Raya died peacefully after a long illness on June 10, 2005. An amazing thing happened while he was near death. A phone call came for him; it was one of the three men from the Ku Klux Klan who had beaten him up many years earlier. The man had traced him down to ask forgiveness for what he had done to him years before in Birmingham. Father Joe of course forgave him; in fact he had forgiven all of his assailants many years earlier, but he reassured the caller that all was forgiven.

Father Raya taught me the importance of joy. He would burst forth with delight whenever he met anyone he hadn't seen in a long time. His joyful smile was his trademark.

His faith and loyalty was an inspiration to everyone who knew him. I will always remember the exuberant way he was able to communicate God's love with everyone he met.

God has created me to do Him some great service.

I am a link in a chain...

A bond of connection between persons.

He has not created me for naught...

If I am in sickness, my sickness may serve Him,

If I am in sorrow, my sorrow may serve Him.

He does nothing in vain,

He knows what He is about.

John Henry Cardinal Newman

9

MR. FRED ROGERS

I got into television because I hated it so, I thought there was some way of using this fabulous instrument to nurture those who watch and listen. One of the most glorious things you can do in life is make the person you are with feel special. Evil in the world would want us to feel as awful as possible about who we are. But Jesus wants us to look at ourselves, and our neighbor and see the best.

Fred Rogers spent his adult life making millions of children feel special. He repeated this message over and over again on his TV program, "Mr. Rogers' Neighborhood," where he entertained and educated children in his own unique way for more than a generation. Fred McFeely Rogers was born in 1928 in Latrobe, Pennsylvania, 40 miles east of Pittsburgh. He studied music composition in college. This helped him to write many of the songs on his TV show.

The first of the "Mr. Rogers' Neighborhood" series began in 1963, and the last original program was aired in 2001, making it Public Broadcasting's longest running program. He won dozens of awards and four Emmy's. A cardigan sweater of his hangs in the Smithsonian. In 2002 President George W. Bush presented him with the Presidential Medal of Freedom, the nation's highest civilian honor, recognizing his contribution to the well-being of children in a career that demonstrated the importance of kindness, compassion and learning.

He tells us how he became an ordained Presbyterian minister in the following interview. From the beginning, "Mr. Rogers' Neighborhood" was deliberately simple and straightforward, largely due to Fred's soothing voice and purposeful actions. Every show began with him taking off his jacket, and putting on a comfortable sweater.

The slow-paced show offered an alternative universe to most of the slick cartoons found in children's programming. He saw his role as more than providing entertainment for children; he said it was a chance to reach youngsters and give them a foundation for a good life.

Here is the interview I did with him in 1994.

JC: Mr. Fred Rogers, welcome.

FR: Thank you, John. It's good to be back again on Christopher Closeup.

JC: The theme song of your TV show, contains the words, "Won't you be my neighbor?" Let me begin by asking why you used those words in your opening?

FR: When I hear words like those, I think the person speaking them cares about me. And I want the children to know that I care about them, all of them. I want them to feel that each one of them is special.

JC: Your new book is entitled *You are Special.* Tell us a little about it.

FR: I've collected lots of quotes and sayings over the last forty years, and they all describe how I want to feel about the person

I am with at the moment. It is one of the most glorious things you can do in life, making the person you are with feel special. Evil in the world would want us to feel as awful as we could about who we are. But Jesus wants us to look at ourselves, and our neighbors, and see the best in them. How wonderful it would be, if in life, we all became advocates rather than accusers.

JC: In other words, promoting the person you're with, not tearing him or her down.

FR: Exactly. That's a wonderful way of putting it.

JC: Do you see your TV work as a kind of ministry?

FR: Yes, I do. Years ago, when I started doing the children's TV show, people suggested that I should take some courses in theology, and I thought that might be interesting. So I began doing it on my lunch hour, and it went on for eight years. Finally they said that I had accumulated enough course credits to get ordained. So to my surprise I was able to become an ordained minister. And then the Church commissioned me to perform my ministry on TV. The goal was primarily to work with families with young children.

JC: How do you select the themes for your show?

FR: Many ideas come from the mail we receive. Who would have thought years ago that we would one day do a whole show on divorce? But children need to know that it is not their fault when their parents separate. Little children tend to think that the world revolves around them. And so consequently anything that happens to them must be because of them; as though the divorce was their fault. They think that it must be "something I did." If a child spills the milk at breakfast and it leads to loud talking between the parents, the child thinks it was his or her fault for making them be mad at one another. They think they caused the breakup.

We try to get through to them that divorce is something that has to do with the adults, and not with them.

JC: Fred, I know you try to get beneath the surface of things. I wonder, can you explain how your work affects the children in your audience?

FR: A lot of people write to us. We get a sense that we are making a difference. I remember a letter I received recently. It was from an adult who had watched the show during his childhood, and he talked of the things he learned from Mr. Rogers growing up. It was very touching.

JC: I heard a story that you were visiting Texas and signing autographs when a little boy came up to you, said his name was Bobby, and you said, "Where do you live, Bobby?" And he answered quizzically, "You know!" Presuming that you had to know where he lived since you came into his home every day on TV.

FR: Yes, there have been many incidents like that. Sometimes they would ask, "How did you get out?" They think I live in that TV set, or somewhere in the TV neighborhood. I met a man who grew up with my show, and who told me he was happy that his children were now watching it as they grow up. He said, "I'm able to see it all again through the eyes of my own children."

It gives us a wonderful feeling to know that we have communicated something on a deep level, something that is lasting.

JC: What has been your greatest satisfaction?

FR: To be able to offer silence through television. There isn't a lot of it out there on the tube.

JC: How do you do that?

FR: Well, there are times when I don't say anything. I might be doing something, and they just watch me. I might be fixing something, or building something, but I don't speak. I used the technique of silence in my book, You Are Special. I think the spaces between the words on a page are sometimes more important than the words themselves. I offer these great quotes, separated by a lot of white space. It gives the reader room to breathe in the meaning. For instance a seminary professor once said, "The only thing that evil cannot stand is forgiveness."

(AFTER A LONG PAUSE, FR. CATOIR ASKED THE FOLLOWING QUESTION.)

JC: I like that. You presume there is an evil power in the world, and you know how to deal with it. You never put on a false front. Fred, is there anything else you try to do for the children?

FR: I think we have to provide them with heroes, like teachers who really believe they have a mission, and that the only reason they are in the classroom is to help the children. I bring on community leaders who see a local gang as nothing more than a cluster of kids trying to make it through life. I bring on policemen and firemen who take care of all of us. Heroes are important in life, because we all need to look up to people. Many of the people we have on our show are unsung heroes.

Most people tend to not get involved, they say things like: "It's not my responsibility to take care of the community!" Or, "It's not my child!" They don't want to take responsibility for helping others. But heroes are the ones who step forward, and take some responsibility for the happiness of others. They want to make this a better world.

JC: So many people are saints and they don't even know it. We are so indebted to them. You bring them to the TV screen every day. Is there anything else you like to do for your viewers?

FR: I try to help the kids to trust their parents. I also want them to believe in the reality of their dreams. Hopefully their dreams will lead them to new challenges, where they can discover whole new worlds of goodness. Ultimately, I want to convince them that they are very special.

JC: Fred, what do you wish for the parents who watch you?

FR: I would want them to listen to the child within each of them, and allow that inner child to know that he or she is unique. Every time I walk into my TV studio I say a prayer, "Dear Lord, let some word that is heard today, be your word, because the rest is merely dross." And I would hope that both parents and children would allow that word to become part of who they are in this world.

JC: Beautiful! Thank you Fred Rogers for this delightful Christopher Closeup visit.

After we finished taping that show at HBO Studios in New York City, the cameramen and technicians all gathered around him, even the executives from upstairs came down to meet him and get his autograph for their children and grandchildren. He quietly spoke to every one of them, and answered their questions.

Fred Rogers died at the age of 74, on February 27, 2003, in his home in Pittsburgh, Pennsylvania, after a brief battle with stomach cancer. His last public appearance was on January 1, 2003, when he served as a Grand Marshal of the Tournament of Roses Parade, and tossed the coin for the Rose Bowl Football Game.

David Newell, a Rogers' family spokesperson, told the Associated Press that Mr. Rogers was exactly as he appeared on TV. "He was genuinely kind, a wonderful person. His mission was to work with families and children; that was his passion and that's exactly what he did from day one."

Fred Rogers is the only non-Catholic in this collection of interviews. I met many other Christian saints not of our faith, but he stands out among them. The great lesson I learned from Fred was humility. Whenever I went to dinner with him a crowd would collect around him. Fred was always gracious and kind.

He will be missed. Thank God the children have his TV reruns.

Twenty years from now
You will be more disappointed
By the things that you didn't do
Than the ones you did do.

Mark Twain

10

JOHN CARDINAL O'CONNOR

If the Church is going to do its job, it has to address public policy issues. People will tell us that they want us to preach the fundamentals of Catholic teaching. They want us to preach sound doctrine, and sound moral teaching, but you get the impression that some of them want you to do that in a vacuum.

Cardinal O'Connor was Archbishop of New York from 1984 until his death on May 3, 2003. He was never shy about telling anyone exactly where he stood on any issue. Ordained a priest in 1945, he was consecrated a bishop in 1979, and elevated to Cardinal in 1985. In between, he served as Chief of Chaplains for the U.S. Navy, attaining the rank of Rear Admiral.

When I was stationed in New York, I used to help at St. Patrick's Cathedral, offering Mass and hearing confessions once a week; I did that for five years. The Cardinal had his residence there, and a few times a year he shared a meal with the priests who staffed the Cathedral.

On the very day he was installed as New York's new Archbishop, the local ABC-TV station asked me to interview him at his residence, in a remote broadcast. The studio was about two miles away. It was a daunting experience. The Archbishop had a reputation of being both a tough, and also a compassionate leader. So my first question was about how he managed to balance these apparently different characteristics.

He replied quickly, and put an end to that particular discussion, "I see no conflict!" His answers were typically curt, and certain.

A few years later I interviewed him on my own program, "Christopher Closeup." Here is the transcript of that show.

JC: In January of 1984, Pope John Paul II appointed you as the new Archbishop of New York. How did you react when you heard the news that you were going to be the Archbishop of the New York Archdiocese?

CO: I was absolutely stunned. I told this story before, but you might find it interesting. The word of this sort comes through the Papal Nuncio, in Washington. At the time I was very happily ensconced as the Bishop of Scranton, Pennsylvania. I had been there only seven months, and thought I'd stay there until I died.

The Nuncio called me one day, and he chatted for about ten minutes, inconsequentially. We were laughing about this, that, and the other thing. And then he stopped for a moment, and he said, "By the way, the Holy Father has appointed you Archbishop of New York."

JC: Just like that?

CO: I was shattered. My first feeling was one of just overwhelming regret and sorrow at the idea of leaving Scranton. And then my second feeling, naturally, was one of being overpowered and scared to death of what would lie ahead.

JC: On March 19, 1984, you were installed as the Archbishop. And that was a very special day for New Yorkers. What was it like for you?

CO: I was more than overwhelmed. May I read you one brief letter? A young lad was kind enough to write to tell me that we shared the same name: John J. O'Connor. There is a slight discrepancy in our ages. Here it is:

My name is John J. O'Connor, too. I'm ten years old. I come from Visitation School. I am becoming an altar boy this year, and you are becoming an archbishop this year. I hope I can be just like you when I grow up. I like to help people when I see them in trouble. I would love to go to St. Patrick's Church just to see you become an archbishop. The day when you become an archbishop is my granddad's anniversary, and the day before my birthday. I love you. (Signed, "John")

You know what made such an impact on me when I read that letter? It was not the mere coincidence of names. It was one sobering sentence – *"I hope I can be just like you when I grow up."*

For years I've been asking parents, "Do you want your children to be just like you when they grow up?" If not, why not? And now I had to ask myself would I really want young John J. O'Connor to be just like me when he grows up? If not, why not? It's a sobering question indeed.

For to the degree that I can merit young John's trust, I will be the kind of bishop I should be to the magnificent people of New York.

(THE CARDINAL THEN TURNED TO THE CAMERA AND SAID TO THE VIEWER):

I need you very much. I need your strength. I need your wisdom. I need your counsel. Above all, I need your love. How much, how very much, I will love you in return. God bless you.

JC: Those were very powerful words, Cardinal. You speak with some emotion about love. Let's talk about your spiritual leadership in that context.

What in your judgment characterizes the spiritual responsibilities of an archbishop?

CO: I think I'm still trying to identify them so that I could adopt them and grow into them, to a degree at least.

I feel the need of praying far more than I ever felt before. I've always recognized the criticality of prayer, but in this current situation, I find myself just increasing the amount of time that I formally pray, and the amount of time that I am reflecting, not simply on problems, but on the need for Divine assistance.

In terms of the leadership itself, spiritual leadership, I think that there are two factors that are absolutely indispensable. And when you honestly, sincerely believe in the worth and dignity of every human person as made in the image and likeness of God, there can't be any shame about that, and you can't make any exceptions.

You have to – if you believe that the unborn is a person – then you have to have the same concern for the unborn as you do for the person in the wheelchair, the handicapped, the elderly, those in the streets, the homeless, those in our soup kitchens, black, white, men, women. So that, I think, just has to pervade everything that you do. You have to ask that question about every plan you initiate, every action in which you engage.

Who am I dealing with? Why am I doing this? What is this for? Here in New York we have almost two million Catholics, with some seven and a half million people in the city, and millions more in the Archdiocese in upstate New York, and every one of them is a person with human dignity. That is my passionate conviction.

And the other thing is that you really have to love, and it has to be a love that goes beyond mere liking; it has to be more than merely not being repelled by people who don't like you. You can't simply cringe under criticism, or run away, if you are under siege just because you attempted to articulate the truth.

You have to say to yourself "I still have to love those people," because your very critics who might, almost ferociously, disagree with you, are still persons. They are still made in the image and the likeness of God.

These are the things that I try to use as criteria for being an effective archbishop. Whatever other mystical, magical qualities or charismatic gifts a spiritual leader should have, I don't know, because I don't pretend to have them.

JC: You were ordained a priest back in 1945. Why did you decide to be a priest? Can you tell us something about your dreams as a young man? Why did you become a priest? What were your hopes?

CO: I think for any of us, it would be difficult to say what started us off on the road to becoming a priest. I have a wonderful family, a Catholic family. The Church was important in the family, but I have to say that there wasn't any intensity about the Church. The rosary was said at home. We were taught to say our prayers in the morning and at night. Part of the time I went to Catholic school, part to public school.

But I think that more than anything else, the Christian Brothers in high school were the ones who guided me, and who, if the potential was already there, actualized it. Their example, their self-discipline, and maybe the fact that they had vocation exhibits made a difference.

So I just made a decision to enter the seminary. But really, my first desire was to become a Maryknoll missionary in some exotic place when I was a kid. I've been to most of those places since then, and they...

(LAUGH!).

JC: They were not very exotic?

CO: Exactly! They were not very exotic at all. I changed my dream vision when a local parish priest asked me: "What's wrong with being a priest in the Archdiocese of Philadelphia?" I couldn't think of anything, and even though I didn't know anything about being a diocesan priest, I thought that might be all right too. That's what happened.

JC: So you applied to the seminary in your home Archdiocese of Philadelphia?

CO: Yes.

JC: In 1952, you joined the Navy. You were already a priest, and you wanted to be a chaplain. What made you decide to enlist?

CO: Korea was on, and an Archbishop came into Philadelphia – Archbishop O'Hara. He had been President of Notre Dame University, and was then the Vicar General of the Military Vicariate. It was his responsibility in that role to visit armed forces all over the world. He was working with Cardinal Spellman in that job.

Well, as fate or providence would have it, he became the Archbishop of Philadelphia. So he was now my Archbishop. And he was no sooner in the archdiocese than he asked for priests to volunteer because of the critical needs of Korea. Actually, I was teaching at the time. I was working with my first love, retarded children. And I was told that the Archbishop wanted me to establish a center for retarded children. We didn't have one. And I was just delighted with the idea. But then, he asked that priests volunteer for the service, so I just put it to him directly. Do you want me to establish the center, or do you want me to go into the service?

He said, because of the shortage, he would like me to go into the service. He said that when I came back, the retarded children would be waiting. Well, later he kept asking me to stay in the service when my time was up... to stay and to stay. The Archbishop kept asking me to stay, and so I did for 27 years.

JC: That was a long time.
CO: Yes.

JC: You saw combat during those years?
CO: Yes. Not a great deal, but I did.

JC: Well, what did that experience – the military and the experience of war – teach you about war and peace, a topic the bishops have addressed quite a bit in the last year?
   CO: I think that anybody who's lived in a hole in the ground, covered with mud; anybody who has crawled through a jungle; anybody who has ministered to men that are dying, just splattered with blood; anybody who sees the horrible destructiveness, it just repels, it tears you apart.
   And despite the stereotype that military people are warmongers, I don't find that to be true. Is there one here or there? Well, you can say that. But you want to do everything that you can to bring our men home.
   You passionately believe what Pope John Paul II says, that peace is possible. You nevertheless know that in the human condition, there is going to be at best an uneasy peace, and that conflicts are going to continue to break out in the world.
   So you want to do everything you can to try to prevent the probability of war, but recognizing the probability, you want to do everything that you can to reduce the horrors of war.
   I think that this is what the American bishops were about in the development of the document *"The Challenge of Peace: God's Promise and Our Response,"* the pastoral letter on war and peace.

JC: This document hit the news recently, didn't it? It was on the cover of *Time*?

CO: Yes.

JC: What was your role in writing it?

CO: I hope that my role was to attempt, as intensely, as resolutely as anyone on the committee, to come out with a document that would express the horrors of war, would do everything it could to advance the course of peace, help prevent the outbreak of war, and reduce the horrors of war if it occurred.

Now there was so much emphasis on the horrendous possibilities of nuclear war, and this emphasis was certainly deserved. There were times when we disagreed on approaches which should be taken. The question was always in the minds of everybody on the committee: What will best advance the cause of peace? There were times when I felt that taking this particular path, or that particular path, would advance the cause of peace better than some of my confreres on the committee.

I know, of course, realistically, I've been frequently depicted as the Genghis Khan on the committee, the militant one, and that I resisted efforts to call for a nuclear freeze, and so on. I just think that that was an unbalanced evaluation. I think that each one of us had very strong convictions about the same objective: How can we best assure peace, or a reduction in the horrors of war?

Naturally my experience of 27 years in uniform made me look at things in a particular fashion. Others looked at things in another fashion. There were never any disagreements about the objective. I hope that each member of the committee contributed to eventually bringing about balance in the document. I think that it was quite possible that if any one of us on the committee had written the totality of the document (I personally wrote a number of pages urging that we give much more of a hearing to those who advocate non-violent resistance, and urging that we be much more sympathetic to pacifists)... I think that if any one of us, however, had written the totality of the document, it would have been a less balanced document than it is now.

JC: We didn't mention yet that you had become the Chief of Chaplains in the U.S. Navy, and that you retired with the rank of Admiral.
CO: Yes.

JC: All of this thrust you into the politics of war and peace, which means that when you speak on these topics all kinds of things happen in the news. What is your estimate of the role of the Church in the political order?
CO: Well, I think that we have an absolute moral imperative to address public policy. What issues are there of any significance that affect human beings, that don't have moral and/or religious implications?

Right now I am engaged, for the Archdiocese of New York, in a major drive for the homeless, the ill-housed – the homeless, I mean the street people, the ill-housed people who live in horrible housing, or far too costly housing. I am concerned about hunger and unemployment. Now there is a moral dimension to every one of these, because we are talking about God's people. We are talking about persons of dignity and worth. And when I go out on the streets, and when I see people out there, whether they are there because of de-institutionalization, or whether they are there for whatever reasons, they are there, they are cold, they are hungry, they are in trouble, they are confused, many of them.

And if I say, "Well, I am the Archbishop of New York, so I must address this," I dare not be quiet because I can be accused of intervening in the political system. For instance, if I make the point that everybody else makes, that we have thousands of people on the streets, then I could be accused of saying that the

Mayor isn't doing his job, or that the Governor isn't doing his job, or the Federal Government isn't doing its job, and so on.

But, I think that perhaps some Catholics actually want you to teach behind closed doors, in a vacuum, and not address real issues. And certainly there are people who disagree with you, in the media as well, although I am a great supporter of the media. I am very, very grateful for the fantastic opportunities given me by the media to reach so many people.

But there are some people who, you know, if you dare disagree with them, then it's not merely that you as a citizen are raising your voice in protest against the destruction of human life, or violation of human life, or the exploitation of human life; it's that you, as the Archbishop of New York, are daring to interfere in the political process. I think that's nonsense.

Look at international issues, and I won't take too much of your time on this – look at some of the most critical international issues today. Look at the situation in the Middle East. How can you separate that from religious issues? We are told that we have Christians fighting non-Christians. We have Christians fighting among themselves. We have non-Christians fighting among themselves. This is allegedly a major element of what's happening.

In Ireland, for instance, you know, the terrible discrimination in Ireland. There's a major religious element there in all that.

Now, are we, as so-called religious leaders supposed to stand by and say these are all economic issues, these are all sociologic issues, and the Church has nothing to say about them? That's foolish.

JC: This brings us back to what you were saying earlier, that if your premise is to defend human rights, and to take an interest in individual dignity, then you're going to be involved in all these issues.

In your very first talk, in your installation, I noticed that you stressed that people were basically good. Cab drivers and waitresses talked about you and said that you had reached them. Some I talked to were surprising; they almost seemed shocked that somebody like an Archbishop would affirm their goodness.

Why is it so difficult for people to believe in their own goodness? Why do you address that topic so often?

CO: I think that's an awfully important question, and I'm glad you made comment on the reaction among cab drivers and others. And I still find it wherever I go. I believe it so intensely. I believe that, again, everybody is made in the image and likeness of Almighty God. There's tremendous potential in them, and I think we have to keep telling people they are good, or they are not going to recognize their potential for greatness, for being what they could be, for being what God intended them to be.

If you tell people they're no good, they're rubbish, it's wrong! They have enough to discourage them already. I couldn't blame them if their response is, "Well, if we are that bad, then there is no point trying."

I think there has been so much in our society that has contributed to making people feel that they are basically no good, that they are not only unloved, but unlovable as well.

JC: You're talking about sinners, as well, aren't you?

CO: I'm talking about sinners, and I'm talking about people who think they are sinners and they are not sinners. I'm talking about people who think that everything they do is a sin. And that's not because the Catholic Church has overemphasized the concept of sin, as many people have unjustly alleged. I don't think that's it at all. I think they've been given a sense of worthlessness.

Look at the kids who are abandoned. Look at the huge number of broken marriages. I realize that there are many lonely and difficult marriages, and it's awfully hard for people to live together, but all this has to be considered. Every time a marriage breaks up, do the kids ask themselves with an unconscious uneasiness, "Didn't my parents love me enough to stay together, to try to take care of me?" So, so many things contribute to a sense of worthlessness.

JC: I'd like to ask an important question. For you, Cardinal O'Connor, who is Jesus Christ?

CO: Oh, that's the critical question for all of us to answer. For me Jesus Christ is the Son of God, absolutely, in whose image I was made and you were made, and everybody I know was made.

JC: Archbishop, thank you for being our guest on "Christopher Closeup." We hope we will see you back again soon. God bless you.

CO: Thank you so much.

Cardinal O'Connor was a pro-life champion. What I learned about holiness from him was the importance of giving Christian witness, and speaking out on issues involving the protection of human rights, and of bringing the mind and heart of Christ to the public forum. He always spoke the truth with love.

Show me thy ways O Lord,
teach me thy paths.
Lead me in thy truth...
on Thee do I wait all the day.

Psalms 25:4, 5

11

FATHER BERNARD HÄRING

*One of the most beautiful treatises in the theological Summa
of Saint Thomas Aquinas is the one on epikeia (IIa, IIae,
120). St. Thomas holds with Aristotle that it is vicious to
apply human laws mechanically, without respect to the
dignity of man and the common welfare.*

Father Bernard Häring was born in Germany in 1912. He was
considered by many to be the greatest moral theologian of the
twentieth century. No one did more to move Catholic moral
teachings from its earlier rigid legalism to a view grounded
in compassion and love. Häring was a member of the Congregation of the Most Holy Redeemer, called the Redemptorists.
He received his doctorate in theology from the University of
Tübingen, where he studied under such great theologians as
Karl Adam, Theodore Steinbuechel, Otto Schilling, and Romano
Guardini.

His practical experience included four years as a military
chaplain in World War II, most of the time on the Russian front.
His teaching career was impressive: Professor of Moral Theology
and Pastoral Sociology at Gars, Germany (1947-1950), and later
at the Alphonsian Institute in Rome (1950-1957). In 1953 he also
directed the pastoral-sociological "European type" mission in

West Germany, and taught Pastoral Theology in Germany, France, Austria, and Switzerland.

After Pope John XXIII began to praise his view of moral theology in public audiences, Father Häring was made a consulter to the Second Vatican Council. His three-volume work, *The Law of Christ*, was published originally in German in 1954 and later translated into fifteen languages. It signaled a new approach to moral theology. When the birth control encyclical, *Humanae vitae*, was released by Pope Paul VI in 1968, Häring was in the United States and issued the following statement:

> *Whoever can be convinced that the "absolute" forbidding of artificial means of birth control, as stated by this encyclical, is the correct interpretation of divine law, must earnestly endeavor to live according to this conviction. Whoever, however, after serious reflection and prayer is convinced that in his or her case such a prohibition could not be the will of God should in, inner peace, follow his/her conscience and not thereby feel her/himself to be a second-class Catholic.*

I met him a few weeks after the encyclical *Humanae vitae* was issued. Fr. Häring had come to the U.S. to give a retreat to the Missionary Sisters of the Immaculate Conception. I was living on their grounds, on the campus of Tombrok College at the time. I was teaching a course on the History of Religions there.

On the first night that Father Häring arrived, I expressed my concerns at dinner about the new encyclical. Most priests were confused about how to implement it, because the laity were quite disturbed about it.

Here is an excerpt from that conversation.

JC: Does the new papal encyclical trouble you at all?

BH: No, I think the laity will make up their own minds about it, and in a few months the storm will be over, and it will be just another document.

JC: But there are those who will not be comfortable with the idea of ignoring it. Some bishops are asking priests to take an oath to preach, teach and counsel according to this ideal, that no sexual contact should be made that is not open to procreation.

BH: I think this will pass. We must read the encyclical and be respectful of papal authority, but the application of the teaching falls to the conscience of each individual couple.

JC: Somewhere in your writings you condemned modern day Pharisees. How would you define Phariseeism?

BH: In Matthew 15:2-9 the Pharisees were annoyed at Christ's disregard for the fasting laws, and asked Him, "Why do Your disciples transgress the traditions of the ancients?" He responded, *"Why do you transgress the law of God by your traditions? You have made God's law null and void out of respect for your traditions."* He accuses them of *"teaching as doctrine the precepts of men."* In Mark 7:9, we find Christ saying, *"How well do you set aside the commandment of God in order to maintain your own tradition."*

Pharisees tended to enforce the letter of the law, that is the narrowest interpretation of the law. They often considered manmade laws to be equal to divine commands. The Pharisees reacted to situations with legalistic solutions.

JC: The Pharisees reacted with legal solutions? In what way?

BH: The Pharisees were addicted to a deplorable kind of casuistry and delighted in all kinds of petty applications of the law. They persisted in judging human conduct only in the light of their own legal situation, isolating it from the context of the essential law of God, the law of love, and from the real life situation of people in general. We have an interesting example of this in the Dead Sea Scrolls. It was said that if a man falls into a pit on the Sabbath, even if the pit is filled with water, nobody should make a move to free him before the first evening star of the Sabbath arose.

But the Lord rebuked this thinking: *"But if a beast falls into a pit, then you quickly liberate him, and for man, you do not!"* The Pharisees were not seeing the central truth about the Sabbath law; namely, that it was meant, not to restrict man, but to benefit him that he might learn to adore God, the Father of all men, in the community of men.

They took the Sabbath out of context, and judged the situation according to a fixed pattern, without thinking about the wishes of the Father of man. This is a typical example of the kind of estrangement induced by an unrestrained casuistry – the type of thinking, which has tended to blight much of "establishment" thinking down through the ages, and against which the prophets fought so zealously.

JC: How does the question of moral relativism fit into this kind of thinking?

BH: The Pharisees go to one extreme, and those theologians who espouse a form of situation ethics go to the other extreme. We have to find a gospel solution to these two extremes. "Situation ethics," a system of thought which taught that there are no unbreakable principles, became popular in Germany and France in the 1930's. In the English-speaking world, Joseph Fletcher of the Episcopal Theological School in Cambridge, Massachusetts, is one of the outstanding advocates of this new view.

In a debate I had with him at Yale University, I asked him about his opinion that there are no absolute principles. I brought up the prohibition against rape and asked, "Can there ever be a situation where rape is good in itself?"

He replied, "Of course. Since there are no unbreakable principles, why would rape not be justifiable in some set of circumstances, perhaps motivated in some way by a loving concern?"

JC: Was he serious?

BH: Yes, of course he was. Situation ethics holds that there is no principle that is absolute, and therefore cannot be broken.

JC: That viewpoint is absurd.

BH: Of course. It is an extreme.

JC: But how does this relate to the Pharisees, and the Church's teaching authority?

BH: Today, almost everyone agrees that in past centuries the Catholic manuals of moral theology maintained too many "absolutes," especially with regard to liturgical matters.

One example is the teaching that *under no circumstances whatsoever* could the Eucharist be celebrated without using an altar stone consecrated by a bishop. They even went so far as to prohibit priests of the Latin Rite, in a very unbending and absolute way, from celebrating Mass on an altar of an Eastern Catholic Church where, instead of an altar stone with relics, they used an antimension (a linen containing relics).

Today, it seems ridiculous that intelligent and open-minded men had to go through a crisis of conscience and obedience until they realize that such things cannot be absolute.

In June 1941, a few weeks before the beginning of Germany's war with Russia, I was in the medical corps, stationed along the Russian frontier. I was with four other young priests. I told them that, in spite of the law of the Hitler regime forbidding all religious activity, we could possibly offer the Eucharist for believers in the Army. These four men all were generous enough to risk being jailed for such illegal activity. But when they discovered that they would have to celebrate Mass, either without an altar stone or an antimension of the Eastern Church, there was real trouble. Finally, I told one of them that I would take on myself all the "mortal sins" we might commit in serving the soldiers. They finally agreed, and we managed to give hundreds of men the Eucharist. To deprive them of the Eucharist, just because of the lack of an altar stone, would have been a graver sin.

One other case comes to mind. In 1950, during a home mission in a West German diocese, a couple came to the missionaries to explain their case. Forty years before, the husband had married a girl who did not know the meaning of marriage and refused intercourse. The priest whom the man consulted at the time told him that his marriage could be annulled, and the man then obtained a civil divorce. However, he never got the annulment, although he tried, and went through a series of frustrating procedures only to be denied.

Finally he married another Catholic girl civilly. Since he was now living in a place where no one knew of his first marriage, they hoped to receive Holy Communion without giving scandal. They approached the mission priest, assuring him that for the past fifteen years they had lived "as brother and sister," that is without having sexual intercourse. They had gone to Mass and said the rosary together almost daily, but they had never received Communion, and now they were asking if they could finally be admitted to Communion, at least during the mission that was taking place there.

The diocese office gave this response:

Since by our orders issued in 1941 we are bound to grant such requests only if both persons have passed their sixtieth year and since this wife is only fifty-nine years old now, we are unable to grant the request. They cannot receive the sacraments.

The officials felt bound to enforce a law to the letter, and nothing else mattered! It seems chilling, doesn't it.

The basic reason for such a law could only be to prevent scandal. But in this case, by keeping the "law," they provoked scandal, since people would now wonder why the couple had not received Holy Communion during the parish mission. So the words of God were disregarded, *"Whoever comes to Me, I will not cast him away."*

Instead of looking into the meaning of the law and the special needs of the persons involved, as well as the common good of the Church, these officials transgressed the most fundamental law of God because of their determination to apply the law mechanically.

JC: What remedy do you see in protecting against the spirit of legalism in the Church?

BH: We need to examine our consciences on this point, and ask ourselves whether we are sometimes attempting to protect ourselves by not being accused of breaking the law. By applying it mechanically in all cases the officials feel they have proceeded correctly and could not be blamed, even if it did seem cruel.

The whole matter with regard to absolutes and the absolute application of laws has to be restudied according to a personalistic frame of thought. The decisive criterion must be the scale of values: the person's sincerity, the good of the persons involved, and their growth in the capacity to reciprocate love.

Here's another case. In World War II, we were taking care of many unfortunate children. Under Hitler's orders, the SS men came to the orphanages and asked, "How many children do you have who are afflicted by disease, or are mentally retarded?" In a few cases, the nuns, in great distress but with literal "truth," answered the spoken question, and the unfortunate children were taken off to the gas chambers. Other nuns answered simply, "We have no such children," and that was the truthful answer to the real question that had been asked, "How many children do you have that we can take off to the gas chambers?" Because they had no children whom they wanted to send to the gas chambers they said, "We have no such children," a truthful response.

Out of an intelligent sense of responsibility, these nuns did what is easily explained by anyone familiar with the philosophy of communication. They realized that not only the words, but also the context can change the substance of a communication. They interpreted the context of the presence of SS men, and their evil intention, as well as the political climate of the times, and rightly answered the question that had actually been asked.

So language must be studied. What is language? It is a communication between persons. In this case, the SS men did not want genuine dialogue, but cooperation with their wicked designs. The only real moral truth at issue was whether or not the sisters would cooperate with their evil intentions.

JC: Circumstances always must be considered in judging moral actions.

BH: Yes of course, this is basic to our training in moral theology. If we talk about the morality of an action, we cannot simply label it with a name picked from the dictionary and make a decision on the basis of that name, but we must look to the moral meaning of this particular action according to its motivation and full context.

JC: We have a Divine Commandment which requires us to keep holy the Sabbath. For Catholics that means you must go to Mass on Sunday. However, if you're sick we all know that we are excused. So even on this important commandment there can be exceptions. But what of the other categories?

BH: You cannot bind a person with a moral obligation they will be unable to fulfill because of bodily sickness.

JC: How do you counsel Catholics who have extreme difficulty with the birth control issue?

BH: St. Thomas Aquinas showed us that Aristotle made a major contribution in the human struggle against the constant threat of a legalistic spirit. He insisted that every man-made law can become brutal and unjust if applied in all cases without regard for circumstances. He spoke of *epikeia*, that special virtue of prudence and of realism, which a lawgiver, who is wise and prudent, must have. Such a lawgiver knows that no man-made law, regardless of the excellence of its formulation, can apply to every extraordinary situation in the same way. If he does not realize this, and expects his laws to be mechanically applied in all cases, he is an unwise and imprudent man, unfit to make laws.

According to Aristotle, *epikeia*, which is the sense of exception to the general rule, means that there must also be right thinking on the part of those who implement the law. It is an insult to the lawgiver to think that his laws apply to every situation and to the same degree without exception. Moreover, the authority of the lawgiver can be eroded by a mechanical application of the law without respect for the social welfare.

St. Alphonsus Liguori poses the question whether *epikeia* applies only to man-made laws or even to the formulations of the natural law as well. Surprisingly, he says that it does apply to formulations of the natural law. St. Alphonsus was convinced that, in extraordinary situations, a decision which contradicts a formulation of a natural-law principle can be justified if there is enough evidence that the action is free from malice (*Theologia Moralis*, I, 201). This question becomes actual in day-to-day conflicts of duty. How does this thinking fit into the Church's teaching? Well, if we interpret strictly the declaration of the Holy Office of February 2, 1956, condemning situation ethics, then it would seem that St. Alphonsus was condemned. However, Pius XII declared him the patron saint of confessors and moral theologians. So we can safely accept his thinking as worthy of acceptance.

JC: Do all Church leaders accept epikeia as a valid theory?

BH: Some do not. One of the chief reasons for the present authority crisis in the Church, and why there are so many protests, is that some in authority would like to impose a quasi-mechanical application of Church law on everyone. St. Alphonsus Liguori taught quite clearly that a sense of exception could be applied to all man-made laws, and even to secondary formulations of the natural law.

JC: So you are saying that some Catholic couples could be in good faith when they follow their conscience and marry civilly, that is, even if the marriage is not canonically valid. In other words, an uncanonical marriage is not always sinful.

BH: Correct, the word "always" is too broad. We cannot know God's mind, or overrule His mercy.

JC: Thank you, Father Häring.

Father Häring despised pharisaical thinking. He dedicated himself to defending the dignity of the individual, at the same time, always keeping in mind the common good. Justice tempered with mercy was his primary criteria for interpreting the law. He had the respect of Pope John XXIII, who made him a "peritus," an expert, at the Second Vatican Council.

When they saw the boldness
of Peter and John... they knew
that they had been with Jesus.

Acts 4:13

12

MSGR. JOHN TRACY ELLIS

The thinking of the hierarchy has been profoundly colored by a spirit of secrecy. This has pervaded the Church for centuries. Because of this the bishops are vulnerable to a kind of behavior that is not so much determined by conscious choices, as by the hidden forces of the institution.

The boldness of the late Monsignor John Tracy Ellis was legendary. Perhaps the most outstanding Church historian of the twentieth century, he never hesitated to speak the truth with love.

During the early 1960's Msgr. Ellis was my confessor, while I was studying at Catholic University in Washington, D.C. for my degree in Canon Law. During that time, I got to know him pretty well.

He was born in 1905 in Seneca, Illinois, and died on October 16, 1992. During his professional career he was regarded as the "Dean of American Catholic Historians." As a professor of Church history, he was often seen walking around the campus of Catholic University with a cane and an aristocratic air. His friendly smile was contagious.

John Tracy Ellis wrote twelve books, and hundreds of articles. His most famous work was a two-volume biography of Cardinal Gibbons. I had the privilege of introducing him at the 1972 Canon Law Society Convention, which was held in Seattle, Washington. He gave the keynote address, and no one was disappointed. His topic was on the question of episcopal leadership in the United States. The standing ovation he received expressed more eloquently than anything else the appreciation of the members.

From my own viewpoint, it was more like a holy hour than a keynote address. We were all reminded of the high ideals which brought us to the priesthood. The talk was framed in the form of a letter to a priest friend, who had just been named a bishop.

The opening of the letter gave an accurate picture of the American culture, and how the primacy of profit in our daily lives colors what Americans tend to do, say and think. He then showed how the bishops have imitated the lifestyle of the richest people among us. The most materialistically successful members of society seemed to set the example for many priests.

As you go about people will comment on the kind of car you drive, on the neighborhood in which you live, on the brand of clothes you wear, on the place and form of recreation and amusement you choose to patronize. In brief, the external features of your daily living will count for or against you, and people will take your measure as a churchman who has not succumbed to the multiple and varied lures of the affluent society, and whether, for example, weakness in that respect has betrayed you.

Should this strike you as an exaggerated emphasis, remember that for many Americans there often lingers a faith-recollection from their remote religious training that externals of this kind are incongruous in one called by Christ to follow in the footsteps of the apostles.

He made the news a few years later when he spoke out about the scarcity of American Catholic intellectuals. No one wanted to hear that, but it was true. His forthrightness reminded me of Jesus Christ.

I had the joy of doing a TV interview with Monsignor Ellis years later. I asked him about a lecture he gave in 1969, on the occasion of the 50th Anniversary of Sacred Heart Seminary in Detroit, Michigan. The talk was entitled, "The Priest in an Age of Revolution."

JC: You often quote Teilhard de Chardin, "Nothing is comprehensible except through its history."
JTE: Yes, we don't seem to learn from history.

JC: Please explain what you mean.
JTE: The revolt of the Protestants in the sixteenth century for instance led to the defensive tone and siege mentality of the Council of Trent. The hierarchy tried mightily to stem the tide, and save what was left of the Church. They had lost much of Northern and Western Europe, but they never admitted any fault for the revolt.

JC: How did this play out in the next few centuries?
JTE: The next major upset came from the rationalist movement of the eighteenth century. It sent the Church reeling once again. The Rationalists regarded religion as an outdated crutch, even a hoax, and the exaltation of science began.

Pope Pius VII (1800-1823) went to war against science. In 1789 he resisted the French Revolution mightily. In that year the Holy See erected the Diocese of Baltimore, and made John Carroll its first bishop. At the time, when monarchies were falling in

Europe, and Napoleon's far-flung empire was also beginning to collapse, the Church in America was born. The early beginnings of the American Church were extremely turbulent.

A report sent by John Carroll to Rome, after he had become the first bishop of America, gives a good picture of how difficult the early days had been.

As long as the provinces were subject to the British, the Catholic religion had not penetrated into any but Maryland and Pennsylvania. The laws were most vigorous against the exercise of it; a priest was subject to death for only entering their territories. Catholics were subject to vigorous penalties for adhering to the worship which their conscience approved and were not only excluded from every office under the government, but would hardly have been suffered to remain in any of the provinces if known to profess the faith of Rome (American Catholic Historical Researches, XXIII [1906], 134*)*.

With the Declaration of Independence signed, the new federal government began the great American experiment. It was a plan to bring unity out of diversity; to make one nation, indivisible with liberty and justice for all. The change could not be grasped completely overnight. For Catholics this was the beginning of an entirely new existence. They had been driven out of England in persecutions that had lasted from the time of Henry VIII.

In conformity with diplomatic customs up until that point, in 1788, the Holy See applied to the new American Congress for permission to establish a hierarchy in this country. The reply of Congress was unexpected. They simply stated that such permission was outside the authority of Congress; no permission was needed at all. This was indeed a shock. The Holy See, with perfect freedom, appointed John Carroll of Baltimore, the first American bishop. He was named the Prefect Apostolic of the entire new American Prefecture. (A PREFECTURE IS AN ECCLESIASTICAL TERRITORY, WHICH IS TOO NEW TO BE CLASSIFIED AS A DIOCESE. THIS NEW TERRITORY THEREFORE WAS FIRST PUT UNDER THE AUTHORITY OF THE PROPAGATION OF THE FAITH.)

The papal bull *Ex Hac Apostolicae* was issued November 6, 1789. It did "...declare, create, appoint and constitute John Carroll Bishop and Pastor of the said Church of Baltimore."

All the Catholics in the United States were subjects of the bishop of Baltimore until 1808, when the Holy See divided Baltimore, making it an archdiocese with four suffragan sees: New York, Philadelphia, Bardstown and Boston.

It is not commonly known that the Diocese of Bardstown, Kentucky, included all of what was then the American West. Philadelphia included Delaware, Pennsylvania and the southern part of New Jersey. The New York Diocese took in the entire State of New York plus the northern part of New Jersey.

For 50 more years the Church in New Jersey was divided in two between New York and Philadelphia.

JC: That's very interesting, and not so long ago. Tell us more about the Church in the days of the Revolutionary War.

JTE: Pope Pius VII tightened his reins of power over ecclesiastical life in all its aspects. With the French Revolution raging, the clergy were barely tolerated in France. The new French government wanted to control the priests, so they made all clerics salaried employees of the state, in order to demand an oath of allegiance from them. The Pope reacted to this power-play by threatening to suspend every priest and prelate who took that civil oath. He denounced the new French constitution as schismatic, and denounced the appointment of bishops by the state as a sacrilegious act.

143

JC: What effect did all this have on America?

JTE: You do not need to be a genius to comprehend the fact that the official Church's fear of the future led to an entrenchment of positions, and a closing off of all the channels of communication. Openness and honesty came at a premium. Diplomatic relations were broken off between France and the Church, and this impacted every country in the world.

Pope Pius VII wanted no dialogue with his opponents. In effect it meant that there was to be no compromise in the Church's rejection of the modern world. The Pope actually condemned the building of railroads. This kind of denial of historical progress led to a breakdown in open, honest communications, creating an atmosphere of defensiveness within the Church, where truth, even at the highest ecclesiastical level, was at times compromised. It became almost commonplace to tell lies, in what would quite mistakenly be described as, the interest of religion.

JC: What do you think has been the most serious single weakness of the Roman Catholic Church?

JTE: Frankly, I think it has been the failure of too many of her spokesmen to be open and honest. There have been times, even in today's world, where the covering up of crimes in order to protect the Church has led to terrible scandals. Clearly, the laity can handle any scandal based on human weakness or illness, and still hold on to their faith. They have been well instructed on the distinction between the human element of the Church and the divine. What they can never accept, however, is the toleration of anything that would cover up a scandal.

JC: Thank you, Monsignor John Tracy Ellis.

He was a gentleman and a genuine scholar. I learned much from him about the virtue of courage, and the pursuit of excellence.

Only from the saints,
only from God
does true revolution come.

Pope Benedict XVI

13

FATHER HARVEY STEELE

*In the past, they claimed that a priest's only activity should
be in "saving souls." This seems impossible to me looking
back. The truth is that in those days, the priests, without
realizing it, were a strong bulwark of the rich in their oppres-
sion of the poor. We preached resignation to the victims, and
we praised the generosity of the oppressors when they doled
out scarcely enough for the poor to maintain their lives.*

Father Harvey Steele was born in Cape Breton, Canada, in 1911.
Early in life he learned about the importance of human rights.
His family was dysfunctional, and though his father was a good
man, he was a hopeless alcoholic, a coal miner who tried his
best to be good. Nevertheless the family never knew whether
he would bring home the paycheck or not. Harvey spent most
of his youth trying to compensate for the irresponsibility of his
father. He helped his mother by running a candy store to make
ends meet.

It was my privilege to meet Father Harvey in the Dominican Republic in 1958, when the dictator, Trujillo was reigning
supreme. We dined together with mutual friends, Jim and Bar-
bara Hagen. Jim was a classmate of mine at Fordham University
School of Business. I abandoned business early in life and, at this

point in time, was in my second year at the major seminary, two years away from being ordained a priest.

I was immediately fascinated with Father Steele's idealism. His straight talk about justice was invigorating. This lone missionary with white hair, wearing the customary white cassock of the priests in the tropics, was soft-spoken but he had some strong ideas about social justice.

I was twenty-seven at the time, and I had already served two years in the Army, after being drafted at the end of the Korean War right after graduation. I was an admirer of Dorothy Day, and thought I was more or less liberal in matters of justice, but Harvey Steele's thinking blew me away.

I wanted to know more about him and his work among the poor, so I asked if he would take me on a tour of the villages where he was training local leaders in the cooperative movement. I knew next to nothing about credit unions and consumer co-ops.

He agreed, and the very next day we traveled bright and early over bumpy roads to visit his people. For half an hour we bounced from side to side in the jeep. It was almost impossible to carry on a serious conversation.

At the first village, the natives greeted us with cheers and enthusiasm. There were signs of poverty everywhere, but their tiny shacks, and muddy streets did not seem to dishearten any of them. They washed themselves, and their clothing, in the nearby river. Little boys went about naked. Women carried huge bundles of laundry on their heads as they went about their daily chores.

This was a world quite foreign to me, and I was amazed to see how gracefully Father Steele talked to them in their own language. They would all burst out in laughter from time to time at something he said. The children liked him too, and giggled at his remarks. He was obviously a friend, if not a hero to these people.

At each village, the men gathered around our Jeep like children around an ice-cream truck. Streams of laughter kept bursting forth, but I was not fluent in Spanish, and didn't quite get the joke. I saw them asking questions, and waiting intently for his answers. The women and children gathered on the perimeter of this circle to watch and listen. Harvey was definitely the main event of the day, generating a lot of excitement. I found the whole experience was fascinating.

I had never seen this kind of interaction. It was an experience I shall never forget. A friendship had developed between this priest and his people. Father Steele obviously had a special gift for communicating in any language, but there was something deeper than linguistic skills going on here. There was a level of trust I had not seen before among the missionaries that I knew.

Obviously Harvey communicated his deep desire to help them help themselves. He won their love and respect because he was changing their lives for the better.

In that one day I learned about the power of the cooperative movement. It was not a reform movement as such, it was simply a method of teaching social and economic techniques to raise people out of poverty. Progress, based on common sense and trust was at the heart of it. Friendship and mutual respect were the side benefits.

For years, these people had been living under a ruthless dictator named Trujillo. He had no hesitation to drive them from their farms if he wanted the land to increase his sugar exports, and thus increase his own wealth. They were an exploited people, and there was no one there to help them on the economic level but Padre Pablo, as they called Father Steele.

It was not very long after I returned to the States that I learned that Harvey was in trouble with the dictator. His influence over thousands of the poorest of the poor was viewed with greater suspicion by the civil authorities. He became a potential threat to stability in the land. Trujillo was always ready to remove anyone or any organization from the Dominican Republic, if they posed a threat to him.

The dictator owned four magnificent palaces; Harvey lived in a tiny room, which he did not own. Still Trujillo saw in him a man of power. But Padre Pablo had no interest in power or politics. His only concern was in helping the poor to improve their lot in life.

Because Trujillo could not risk allowing his influence to spread further, he had Harvey arrested at gunpoint, and ordered to leave the Dominican Republic within 24 hours. With that order, fifteen years of hard work had to be left behind.

Fortunately, Trujillo was not able to destroy the legacy Father Steele left behind. The co-op movement he established is still thriving today because of the trained leaders of the community. They kept the dream alive.

At this point in his young life, Fr. Steele had been exiled by force of arms from two countries: China and the Dominican Republic, but that didn't stop him. He soon began all over again in Panama, Central America.

Gary MacEoin, a well-known author, wrote a biography about Father Steele entitled *Agent For Change* (Orbis Books, Maryknoll, N.Y., 1973), in which he tells the whole story of how this young Canadian priest began working in China, only to be driven out during the Japanese invasion in 1942. Harvey then served briefly as an Air Force chaplain in the China-Burma-India theater of operation, but he had to leave China, and after fifteen years in the Dominican Republic, took his dream of helping the poor to Panama.

Harvey and I became friends after my visit with him. Many years later I persuaded him to allow Gary MacEoin to write his story for the world to see.

In fact, he asked me to write the Foreword of that book, which I was very pleased to do. Here is an excerpt.

After my ordination to the priesthood, I got so caught up with Harvey Steele's work, that I tried three times over the years to be released from my diocese to work with him. I was refused permission by two succeeding bishops.

The Diocese of Paterson, New Jersey, had sent me to study for a doctorate in canon law after my ordination. When I returned with my degree they put me in charge of the marriage tribunal. They were not about to let me go off to Panama on some questionable crusade. It was a great disappointment at the time, but I'm sure it was for the best.

I was still able to help Father Steele from afar. I helped him purchase building materials, and shipped books and supplies down to him as he was working to establish his new facilities in Panama City. He created a corporation called the Inter-American Cooperative Institute, and I helped him to raise some money for his mission.

For a long time it distressed me that the official Church never really showed any real interest in his work. A few individual churchmen here and there were kind to him, but the idea of the Church working directly in the socio-economic apostolate never really caught on.

Here is an adaptation of an interview I did with him, long before I was at The Christophers.

JC: Harvey, please comment on your understanding of the Church in the U.S. and the Church in Latin America.

HS: It is a fact of history that religion has always been at the service of the power structures of Latin America, helping to create and maintain the mentality of resignation and passivity characteristic of the poor. In this respect the role of religion in Latin America has been quite different from its role in North America. Arnold Toynbee and other historians have pointed out that modern civilization began with the break away from the medieval disciplines in the last quarter of the fifteenth century. Up to that time, the Catholic Church not only controlled the consciences of the people but also held vast political and economic power.

The modern world was a product of the Protestant Reformation. The new freedoms it introduced coincided with the discovery of the New World and with the opening up of mental horizons to the possibility of even more worlds to discover and conquer. The earth was finally established to be round and not flat. Scientists, bankers, and inventors were all filled with new enthusiasms. Men ceased to be awed by nature or tied down by old superstitions. They became determined to become their own masters.

JC: Could you say a little more about the Protestant Reformation in this context?

HS: The Protestant ethos grew out of the Reformation. Historians regard it as having played a significant part in developing the drive of the early Americans to conquer the wilderness and build a great nation. While John Calvin's role is the subject of some differences of opinion, the prevailing view is that his philosophy was more influential than that of any other religious leader. He insisted that man should be responsible, that he should rely on himself, work hard, be honest, be a good citizen and neighbor. Work was for him the great virtue. God blesses those who work and ensures that they will prosper. Whatever Calvin's original intentions might have been, in practice his teaching was understood as making success the test of virtue. The prosperous businessman was automatically judged a holy man and blessed by God. It was a philosophy that fitted perfectly with the capitalist system, matching many of Adam Smith's economic theories. Such was the attitude of the Protestants who dominated the settlement of North America and who gave it an outlook and a culture that have survived right down to modern times.

Latin America had no experience with this Protestant ethos during its formative period, and even today it is little influenced by it. Catholicism was the state religion in Spanish and Portuguese times, and it still remains the state religion for all practical purposes in most Latin American countries. It is a socially conditioned form of Roman Catholicism, deriving from the medieval Catholicism of southern Europe, very different from the Catholicism of contemporary Germany or Holland. At the popular level, it centered on a series of preoccupations, such as death, health, and immediate temporal concerns. This preoccupation in turn gave rise to a number of practices, prayers to favorite saints, sprinkling of holy water, a system of promises or commitments to perform certain actions or abstain from certain actions in return for a favor one sought from God.

While on the one hand the Christianity preached by the Spaniards freed the Indians from fear by its stress on God's love and mercy, it also tended, simultaneously on the other hand, to compound his traditional fear of nature by introducing new supernatural terrors. God joined nature as an inscrutable and seemingly arbitrary judge of man's fate, a God who was influenced to be more merciful by the Church in all his decision, and who told the individual, through the Church, what he should do and not do. Eternal salvation was singled out as the one important thing, with this life being no more than a time of waiting and watching. Religious teaching stressed the importance of the sacraments as dispensed by the Church in its graciousness. It spoke of supernatural virtues, which were gifts of God and devoted little attention to the natural virtues necessary to achieve development. In contrast to the Calvinist creed, which proclaimed that wealth was a mark of God's favor, the Catholic philosophy preached that God loved the poor. However, it often failed to make the distinction that God loves a man not because he is poor or rich, but because, and to the extent that he is good.

JC: How did the Catholic Church respond to the Calvinist view in the missions?

HS: The Catholic Church officially repudiated this kind of religion. As the Second Vatican Council expressed it in the opening words of its magnificent statement on *The Church in the Modern World,* "The joys and hopes, the griefs and the anxieties of the men of this age, especially those who are poor or in any way afflicted, these too are the joys and hopes, the griefs and anxieties of the followers of Christ." This general statement of position was taken up and applied to its own situation by the Catholic Church in Latin America when its bishops came together in Colombia in September 1968, in a hemispheric assembly opened by Pope Paul VI in person. The outcome of that meeting was the publication of the Medellin Documents as an expression of the consensus of the bishops on the religious, social, economic, and political conditions of Latin America.

These documents contained a 40,000-word call to basic reform, offering the concept of a liberating God to replace the god of private property. They denounced the oppressing power used by institutions to impose violence, the neocolonialism of the national oligarchies, and the external neocolonialism of the "international monopolies and the international imperialism of money," on which the system rests. They specifically list some of the worst effects of all this: the growing distortion of international commerce caused by a decline in the prices of raw materials while those of manufactured goods rise, the flight of capital, the brain drain, the growing burden of debt, tax evasion, and the export of profits and dividends by foreign companies "without contributing the adequate reinvestments to the progressive development of our countries."

According to the Latin American bishops the situation is indeed critical. Here is an excerpt of that document:

Many parts of Latin America are experiencing a situation of injustice which can be called institutionalized violence. The structures of industry and agriculture, the national and international economy, the cultural and political life all violate fundamental rights. Entire peoples lack the bare necessities and live in a condition of such dependency that they can exercise neither initiative nor responsibility. Similarly, they lack all possibility of cultural improvement and of participation in social and political life. Such situations call for global daring and basically renewing change. It should surprise nobody that the temptation to violence should manifest itself in Latin America. It is wrong to abuse the patience of people who have endured for years a situation that would be intolerable if they were more aware of their rights as human beings.

These powerful ideas were issued at Medellin, as the collective voice of all the bishops of Latin America. Subsequently, the bishops in most of the countries have published their own statements, reaffirming what was said at Medellin, and making concrete application to the situation in their respective countries. Unfortunately, however, that is not the resolution of the matter. In Latin America it has always been normal to find an immense gap between verbal professions of position and the real-life fulfillment. And this is such a situation. Church leaders in Latin America have been traditionally allied with the oligarchs, the rich and the rulers. Only a small minority of them has effectively ended that alliance and dependence. Men like Camilo Torres and Che Guevara have died for justice, but there is still great need of men who will live and struggle for it, a task often more difficult than to die for an ideal. Small groups of priests in various countries have raised this banner, but justice needs many more defenders, and one can only hope that young men and women in increasing numbers will dedicate their lives to its cause.

JC: Are you urging priests to be revolutionaries?

HS: No, not in the sense of fostering violence. However, in the past, many priests were able to go through life living the role for which they were conditioned in the seminary. The priest had a very specific image of himself. He felt he was justifying his existence by carrying out all the activities traditionally assigned to him.

After the Second Vatican Council, it became increasingly difficult for priests to live with this kind of rationalization. They find it more difficult to justify the celebration of the Mass or the conferring of baptism or the other sacraments if the purpose is simply to perform a social function, or even more when the recipients are merely driven by superstition. Yet many of us older priests, both those who are natives of the Latin American country in which they work, and those who have come from outside, do not recognize the extent to which we have also been brainwashed. We continue to see ourselves as fulfilling our total commitment by saving souls, without lifting a finger to help the living person composed of body and soul. We think we can fulfill our purpose by conferring the sacraments on people who have no understanding of the true spiritual significance of the actions we perform for them. Some situations call for action to change the structures that prevent men and women from escaping from the subhuman condition in which they live. I know, because I have been part of that system.

To those of my fellow priests who honestly hold such views, I can only appeal to them to reflect further on the reality of our involvement in causing and continuing the present unjust structures in Latin America. In these times, is it not our right and duty to defend justice, and to place ourselves in the front ranks of those seeking justice?

JC: Thank you Father Steele, those are strong words. May God bless you in all you do.
HS: Thank you.

Father Steele died on April 7, 1999 at the Scarboro Missions Society headquarters, near Toronto, Canada; he was 88 years of age. I remember him saying, *"If I make it to heaven, I think I will be much more active there than I have been in this life. It will be an enjoyable, active life. We will not be burdened with our bodies... it will be so wonderful to be free, with God, and our friends – all is love, all is true."*
Harvey suffered many heart-breaking disappointments. He had a number of political enemies, but his ultimate concern for the poor never wavered. He was a dedicated rebel, and yet in his old age I saw him as a humble, retired priest. He was genuinely pure of heart, and his devotion to Mary was marvelous to behold. He wrote a little book about Mary, the Mother of Jesus, and called it *God's Most Beloved*.

Harvey was a man of deep faith. I never met a priest who lived out his beliefs with such passion. Like Jesus he had little patience with those who were "lukewarm," when it came to helping the poor.

Then I saw another angel, flying overhead,
sent to announce the Good News of eternity
to all who live on earth, every nation,
race, language and tribe.

Revelation 14:6

14

MOTHER ANGELICA

In her own words Mother Angelica explains how she managed to be an Abbess and a TV executive at the same time in the years before her retirement:

> *I have incorporated contemplative life and our TV work together. I think one of our witnesses to the world is to make Jesus known and loved. That's why I think our Lord put our network in the most unlikely place, a contemplative house, and a very small contemplative house at that, to prove that prayer and daily life go together, and that the executives, the ditch-diggers, the housewives, the students, all of us together cannot separate God from what we're doing day by day. You see we've isolated our lives, our states in life. We seem to say, "Over here is our life, over there is our God," but we have to give Him homage with our entire life.*

Mother Angelica was the founder and Abbess of Our Lady of the Angels Monastery, originally established in Irondale, Alabama, and now an hour away in Hanceville, Alabama. She was born Rita Rizzo in Canton, Ohio in 1923. Her father abandoned her family when she was about three, leaving her to be raised in poverty by a sick mother who suffered from suicidal depression.

As a result, little Rita became a sickly child. She had a nervous condition, which was described by the doctors as a serious stomach disorder.

To everyone's amazement, she was healed of this disorder through prayer, and eventually became a contemplative nun who became the founder of her own monastery.

I met Mother more than twenty-five years ago when she was just starting her television ministry. In fact I was her replacement on "Mother Angelica Live" a few times when she was traveling. I supported Mother in her struggle to keep the Catholic Communicators from joining an ecumenical venture called VISN.

Though I was in favor of interfaith activities, this plan, as it was presented, placed us at a disadvantage. We saw VISN as an ecumenical venture that would require so much ecclesiastic tact that it would have eventually led to the watering down of Catholic teaching. It also had the potential of limiting the time allowed on air of Catholic TV programming. The story of this conflict is mentioned in Mother's fascinating biography, written by Raymond Arroyo, entitled *Mother Angelica - The Remarkable Story of a Nun, Her Nerve and a Network of Miracles* (Doubleday, 2005).

I am mentioned briefly on p. 210, in these words:

> *Mother Angelica, Father Catoir of The Christophers, and others feared that once cable operators embraced VISN, they would consider their religious-broadcast obligations fulfilled.*

Mother later on in her career also created a worldwide short-wave radio station, which is a direct broadcast satellite service. She has a radio network, an internet site (www.ewtn.com), and a publishing arm, making EWTN the largest media network in the world.

This extensive outreach is something of a moral miracle, given that she operates on a non-profit basis. Her whole life has been a series of miracles. How she managed to integrate all this electronic, high-tech activity into her highly disciplined life of prayer is anyone's guess, but she did it.

From humble origins, Mother Angelica became the C.E.O. of the world's leading television ministry. Her TV station alone is now available to millions of households in 110 countries.

The following interview with Mother was taped at HBO Studios in New York City in 1982, only two years after she opened her TV Network.

JC: Mother, welcome. You are wearing many hats these days, where does all your energy come from?

MA: From prayer, certainly. But I must say, I wonder myself you know. We just keep going and I'm not very well, and my sisters, thank God, tell me, "We can't keep up with you now, Mother, imagine if you were healthy."

I also feel the power of the network helping me, EWTN, is a prayer family. I think that's where the energy comes from, a lot of people are praying for me. Without that there is no energy.

I don't have much time during the day for regular prayer outside of our liturgical prayer. And so I get up very early, sometimes 4:30 or 5:00 in the morning. Then we pray the Divine Office, which is the prayer of the Church, with the psalms and readings, followed by Mass. Then we have breakfast and I give a one-hour lecture to the sisters every morning to feed our souls with a deeper spirituality, from Scripture or from spiritual books.

Around 10 o'clock I go down to the network and I'm either producing a show or doing the business of the network. After lunch I have my hour of adoration before the Blessed Sacrament and then we have more work. The sisters help me with the direct mail system.

JC: May we go back to your early life. When did you decide to become a nun, and how did that come about?

MA: Well, I'm from Canton, Ohio, and one thing I never wanted to be, Father, was a nun. When I was in school I used to sit behind the nuns. Couldn't see Mass at all. Once you got behind them you were lost. You know, they had the big headwear on. I never wanted to be a nun.

Then I had a very, very serious stomach ailment, and was healed of that, miraculously healed through a novena to the Little Flower.

And I began to realize something. I began to realize that God had a special love for me. I had a very difficult time of it. My mother and father were divorced when I was just about 3 years old. And in those days that was a stigma. It was very, very difficult just to survive. My mother and I survived, but it was very hard.

JC: Were you the only child?

MA: I was the only child. That healing made me know something. It made me realize God loves me. And I began to go to Mass more frequently, make Stations of the Cross after work and I remember standing before the statue at the altar of Our Lady of Sorrows in my little church. And at some point, I knew, you know how you know you know, that I had a vocation.

I tried to enter an active community, but I didn't have the grades. I applied to, and was accepted into the Order of St. Joseph. I loved the Apostolate of the Deaf, and wanted to teach the deaf. Even though I was accepted by the Sisters of St. Joseph, my spiritual adviser thought I had a contemplative vocation.

The contemplative vocation is a vocation in which the soul gives itself totally to God in prayer in an effort to help all mankind. A contemplative goes within, for transformation, in order to help every man, woman and child in the whole wide world. For example, if this studio was totally dark, and had only a 7-watt bulb in it, you would have some light. But if you were to put all the bulbs in this room on, that wattage would give you even more light. If I were to put a million watts in here the light would go beyond this room.

Well, that is a kind of symbol of contemplative life. The soul, as it makes progress in the transformation in Christ, and I'm talking about real change now, I'm talking about transformation into the image of Jesus, then that grace will affect the entire world. We become contemplative to thank God for all the things He does for the millions of people who never thank Him. Thanksgiving – our order is geared towards thanksgiving.

JC: Mother, I notice you are wearing braces on your leg.

MA: You know the Lord has pushed me in everything. I just don't move very quickly. I wear braces because I hurt my spine very badly. Way back, the doctor said I only had a 50-50 chance of walking again. I panicked. Absolutely panicked. And I said to the Lord in my panic, I said, "Lord, you give me the grace to walk and I will build you a monastery myself." And why I said that I have no idea.

JC: You said you and the sisters have a one-hour period of adoration each day. Tell us about that.

MA: Our sisters and I pray between 4 and 5 hours a day. That holy hour is before the Blessed Sacrament, before the Real Presence of Jesus in the Eucharist, for the purpose of thanking Him for the marvelous things He does for all mankind. So during that hour we love Him, we praise Him, we thank Him. My own particular prayer life is kind of different. Being Italian by descent, I'm a little bit more active in my prayer life. I get angry with Him sometimes. I argue with Him. I always wonder whose side He is on sometimes, you know. But anyway that hour is geared towards lifting up our hearts and uniting to God through our Lord, in thanksgiving without all the distractions and the weariness of always asking for things, without saying, "Lord, give me this; I need that."

JC: How long have you been the Mother Superior of your monastery, Our Lady of the Angels?

MA: Since 1962, nearly 20 years before I began EWTN. Religious life was going through a turmoil, an identity crisis. But I don't have an identity crisis. I feel religious life is there to witness to the kingdom that is to come, and the kingdom that is here, in the presence of the Lord. The Lord gave us the essence of religious life in the Gospel when He said, "Love one another." He said, "Grant Father that they may be one as we are one so that the world will know you sent me."

JC: How do you balance the TV work and the prayer life?

MA: Well, you have to learn that there is no difference between our daily chores and our spiritual lives. The two go hand in hand. I am living a life of deep union with God. I love Jesus. And there should be no difference between me being at this point sitting here talking to you, and me praying in my chapel. There should be a union of hearts constantly. St. Paul speaks about unceasing prayer.

I am convinced and I want to convince you and everyone else that holiness can be found everywhere. You know, and I know, that television can be a rat race, a dog eat dog type of work. But in that world we have to have holy people too.

JC: I agree, that's why we're doing what we're doing here. I'm very grateful to hear you articulate this view so well. But how, when you're the leader of a monastery, given the prayer schedule you have, how do you manage to get it all in? How do you juggle it all? It's one thing to dream the dream, another to do all that has to be done to make the dream come true. Your success on TV has really boggled the mind of everybody in the industry. You've accomplished so much in such a short amount of time. Tell us, how big is your network? How did you get it going?

MA: First of all, the outreach or the footprint of our TV signal is from Maine to Hawaii, all of Alaska, Canada, Mexico, and Puerto Rico. So we are capable of reaching every cable system around that area after only two years of operating.

The network was not my original idea. It evolved. And as it evolved God stepped in. The idea began when I was a young sister, I went to Channel 38 in Chicago to record some spots. It was a very, very small studio and I realized it doesn't take a lot of equipment to reach the masses. And I remembered standing in the doorway of that studio and saying, "Lord, I've got to have one of these." And later I thought to myself, how stupid! What would I do with it?

But it just stayed on my mind so much, and I went home. In the process I made a tape which was a total disaster. Oh, it was awful. Then I made another one, and a cable station took it. They asked me to make 60 more for them, and I agreed. In the middle of the series I was taping, I saw that the station was going to air a movie called *The Word.* I knew about the movie and thought it was blasphemous. I got very angry with the management, and told them so.

JC: What kind of movie?
MA: *The Word.*

JC: You thought it was…
MA: Blasphemous!

JC: How so?
MA: It depicted Jesus as some kind of a prophet who got emotionally carried away. It treated Him in a disrespectful way. Well, I was angry about that, and I complained to the manager

who told me to leave the studio. He said, "You're off the air." I said, "Oh no I'm not, I don't need you. I'll build my own studio." That was a big mouth statement. I thought to myself, you idiot, what have you said?

So I went home and that very morning we had a meeting and decided to build a TV studio in the garage. We had 1500 cinder blocks left over from another building we had just built, and I said, "I want to build a studio, but I don't know how to build a studio. I wouldn't know where to begin." And everybody together said, "Use the garage." And I said, "The garage?" I went down there and the fellow was digging the footage, and I told him that I wanted it 10 feet wider and 10 feet longer. He asked what for? And I told him I was going to build a television studio. He almost fell over. He said he didn't know how to build a television studio. I said that's not the point, we're going to build it. And so it began.

And that is how the whole thing began. We built that studio in a garage, for the purpose of providing all the dioceses of the country with inexpensive, high quality, TV production. And we built it. I'm told that we now have one of the most professional, and the best master control rooms of studios anywhere in the country. And that's how it evolved. It evolved because I lost my temper.

JC: Wow! Quite a story. Now that you are on the air, how would you describe the message of your network? And who is your target audience?

MA: The message of our network is to tell the person in the pew, the person in the living room, how to live the Scriptures, how to live as Catholics. We target Catholics. It's all well and good to go to our Church on Sunday, but what happens between Sunday and Sunday? We have the whole week to serve God.

So the network is for the spiritual growth of people. We want to portray on the network a basic spirituality level – we want to show the beauty of different types of spirituality. St. Ignatius' spirituality is one thing, and then there is the Dominican and the Franciscan spirituality, so that people in the pew, with varying temperaments, could pick one out, and begin to live a life with God wherever they are. Also I think we give witness to the idea that God is looking out for dodos.

JC: What do you mean?

MA: To me a dodo is someone, who doesn't know that a thing can't be done. The average person out there is angry about a lot of things, but thinks he can't do anything about it. I want to tell him he can. With the grace of God in you and the power of the Holy Spirit in you, you can change the world. St. Paul says, "With God all things are possible."

JC: Do you target the Catholic audience exclusively?

MA: Yes, we are into narrow casting. Narrow casting means we're gearing ourselves to a specific audience. We're gearing ourselves towards a Catholic audience. We're looking for cable systems in predominantly Catholic areas.

However, the network is open for everyone to watch whether you're a Catholic, Protestant, Jew, Muslim or Hindu, you can receive a lot of spirituality from the network.

However, all things being as they are, we target the Catholic audience. We only have four hours a day, we're on from 8 to 12 Eastern time every night. But we plan to expand on that.

JC: Where does the money come from?

MA: God's providence. I don't know any more than you do. It's a scary way of living and a scary way of doing anything. We never know at the beginning of every month where it's coming from, and it costs us about $200,000 a month to keep that place going; we have to rent transponder time in order to broadcast our signal.

JC: $200,000 a month?

MA: Every month. And sometimes we begin a month with only $600. I don't want RCA to know about that because we owe them money, so don't tell them, but that is really how we do it. We trust in God's Providence. We are capable of reaching about 3,000,000 people right now. That is our potential audience.

But you know people flick that dial. Who knows who's watching it? I believe that Jesus would die for one person, so I can build a network for one person. And I want the whole world to watch it.

JC: You know getting back to the practical question of finances, I'm not at all surprised to hear you say that God provides it all, and has done so from the beginning. The Christophers have survived basically on the same kind of trust. We receive nothing from the Church or State. We receive everything from the people who believe in what we're doing. They see our good works. I understand when you tell us that you have survived by trusting God.

What you have been able to do in just a couple of years boggles the imagination. We're very proud of you.

MA: Well, thank you. But you see before the TV ministry came along we had been giving little books away since 1973. We built up a little mailing list sending these pamphlets out every month to these people. And they became the original source of our funding. The Lord Himself inspired this.

I've got to tell you about faith. I want to tell everybody what faith is to me.

Faith to me is one foot in the ground and one foot in the air with a queasy feeling in your stomach. That's faith. It's uncertain sometimes. It's negative. It's anxious. It's frustrating, and it gets you angry. You know I get so angry at the world, at my crew, at my sisters, even at the Lord, but for me that's all part of faith.

JC: To you faith is courage. It takes great courage to step out and trust the Lord enough to take action, knowing that He will help you.

MA: Trust is the eighth gift of the Holy Spirit, but don't tell anybody I said that. I love to confound the big shots that don't know how we do it. When they ask, "Do you have a budget?" I say, "I don't believe in budgets." Then they just go away totally frustrated.

But they're in business, you see. They should have a budget. I'm not in business. I'm doing the Lord's business. Let me explain something to you.

A man called me up and he said to me, "Mother, I don't think you're running that place right." And I said, "Oh, really?" He said, "No, I think you need a budget." And I said to him, "What's a budget?" And so he explained a budget. I said, "Now let me see if I understand. You're saying that I should decide at the beginning of the year that I should spend $100,000 on programming and then I run around and get $100,000 and that's my expense. Is that right?"

He said, "Yeah, that's right, that's a budget." I said, "But what happens if God was to give me $400,000? I just lost $300,000, and that would break my heart."

JC: You keep the door open so God can give you a little more...

MA: You know, I hope I'm halfway sensible about this thing, but I believe that in the Gospel when the Lord said to His apostles, and I'm not talking about business now, I'm talking about the apostolate, when the Lord said, "I send you out with no coppers in your purses," He wanted them to trust Him. Here are the apostles, 12 ignorant laymen. The Scripture says, "They were sent out to found a church on nothing."

JC: They did it on trust. Let me apply this thinking to the question of a vocation. If a young man or woman might be contemplating a vocation to the religious life, but who is filled with fear at the thought that they might fail, or that they are not worthy, what would you say to them?

MA: I would say, you have to develop a theology of risk. If you want to do something for the Lord, you want to give yourself to the Lord, just do it. Do whatever you feel needs to be done. Even though you're shaking in your boots, and are scared to death, take that first step forward. The grace comes with that one step, and you get the grace as you step. Being afraid is not a problem. It's doing nothing when you're afraid, that's the problem.

JC: And we've all learned that the Lord is never outdone in generosity.

MA: That's right. He is never outdone in generosity.

JC: Mother you're a living testimony to that truth.

MA: Thank you.

JC: We're so glad you could be with us. God bless you, and thank you for all your good work.

MA: Thank you.

A little postscript is in order here. Today Mother Angelica's network is bringing the Gospel to a mass audience of 85 million households, in 110 countries throughout the world. That has been quite an accomplishment for a sickly woman who was penniless in the beginning. She only had her trust in God, and that was all she needed. God gave her amazing gifts and miracles in return, to enable her to give Him greater glory.

CONCLUSION

I hope you've enjoyed my conversations with the saints. One of my regrets in writing this book has been the fact that I did not include more lay men and women. They are the unsung heroes of the Church. Unfortunately, there are so many of them, I didn't know where to begin.

The great saints are usually people who don't know that they're saints.

So many wonderful human beings, outstanding in every way, have never been honored in any way, much less been recommended for canonization. They never saw themselves as being especially holy.

Mothers, by the millions, who gave up everything for their children; countless fathers who worked hard year in and year out in order to provide for their families; these good people all deserve the highest praise. The saints work hard building the Kingdom of Heaven on earth, and they are legion.

Looking back over the years, I see a gradual evolution in the ranks of the laity. I recall the various lay movements, which have come and gone in the last century. There is an astonishing untold story here, and it covers the entire twentieth century.

A brief synopsis of the progress made by these wonderful men and women of the laity is in order before I conclude this book.

Lay leadership began to evolve with the social encyclicals of the popes, and the emerging concept of Catholic Action, which was once seen as a participation of the laity in the work of the hierarchy. However, in those days most of the Catholic lay societies, which included sodalities, social clubs, service organizations, and reading circles were divided by gender, and they were used mainly to raise money for Church projects.

1929-1959

The age of the lay apostolate received papal support and encouragement in this period, and there was an explosion of European and American models for lay men and women to seek and find a more active way of serving God and neighbor. Here is a list of the organizations of this period: Young Christian Workers, Young Christian Students, the Catholic Worker, Friendship House, Christian Family Movement, Newman Clubs, Catholic Evidence Guild, Catholic Youth Organization, etc. It was during this period and beyond up until 1977 that Father Keller began inspiring the laity to take responsibility to help make this a better world. He influenced countless men and women to believe that one person can make a difference.

1960-1969

The age of aggiornamento had come, and Catholics struggled to understand the documents of the Second Vatican Council. The concept of the Church as the "people of God," gave the laity new strength. The sacrament of baptism was now understood as including *"the common priesthood of the faithful."* By the late 1960's, renewal movements such as Marriage Encounter, Cursillo, and the Charismatic Movement appeared on the scene, and began to grow. Many devoted Catholics gave their time and talent to help these movements expand.

1970-1980

This decade brought about the emergence of "Lay Ministries." A great debate over the role and status of the laity in the Church included questions such as: Where might the laity best serve? Should they be exclusively in the secular arena or could they also be in the sanctuary? Is there an abiding and inherent difference between the vocation of the ordained clergyman and that of the lay minister? Can the institutional structures of the Church accommodate this expanding vision of the laity's vocation? This debate is still going on, and the tide is turning slowly. The awakening of the sleeping giant of the laity is well under way.

1980-1990

At the end of the century an explosion of lay ministers appear. The laity become responsible for 83% of the parish leadership functions. This includes the youth ministry, the family apostolate, liturgy, musical planning, religious education, spiritual direction, as well as hospital and campus ministries. This great flood of lay ministries included both volunteer and salaried positions. Ministry became a buzz word for everything the laity attempted. Catholic magazines coined the phrase, "the clericalization of the laity." Some, in a cynical turn of phrase, called these ministers, "professional Catholics." There was fear in high places that they would usurp the role of the priests.

In 1987, the Synod on the Laity was considered a failure by many observers. For instance, Peter Hebblethwaite, a writer for *The New York Times*, noted that *"It was a Synod that expired quietly; unloved, unmourned, and largely unreported."* The reason for this has still not been adequately diagnosed. However, the rapidly shrinking clergy is a fact of life. The priesthood has reached a median age of sixty. That means that the growth of lay leadership in the Church can only be a providential blessing. The laity has come of age.

1990-2006

The new emphasis in Catholic circles is on the word "collaboration." We need one another, and yet some confusion still seems to exist over the roles of priests, vis-a-vis the laity, as well as the role of married deacons vis-a-vis the pastor. The growing priest shortage has created a new urgency for closer and closer collaboration between the bishop and his people. Some are calling for a new model of parish life, but no one seems to agree on what shape that model should take.

It is clear that God is calling more and more of us to become saints in these troubled times. We should be open to the saints among us. As you have seen, the saints come in different shades and sizes, and they differ widely in their point of view.

Indeed, the saints are the hope of the future. They march in and disturb the peace with the power of their convictions. The laity are producing more and more saints. They are on the move, and they are much needed if the Church is to survive and thrive in the years to come.

I find this whole mysterious process of interacting with God so exciting. My hat goes off to everyone who is building up the Kingdom, the laity as well as all the deacons, priests and bishops who have worked so hard to make this a better Church and a better world. May God bless all the unsung heroes, each and every one.

May the Lord bless you all for everything you do to build up the Kingdom of God on earth.

Thank you for sharing your time. I pray that the Lord will be your strength and your joy in the days and years ahead.

ST PAULS

This book was produced by ST PAULS, the publishing house operated by the Society of St. Paul, an international religious congregation of priests and brothers dedicated to serving the Church through the communications media.

For information regarding this and associated ministries of the Pauline Family of Congregations, write to the Vocation Director:

Vocation Director of the Society of St. Paul
2187 Victory Blvd., Staten Island, NY 10314

Phone us at (718) 865-8844
E-mail: vocation@stpauls.us
www.stpauls.us

That the Word of God be everywhere known and loved.